# Echoes of Light

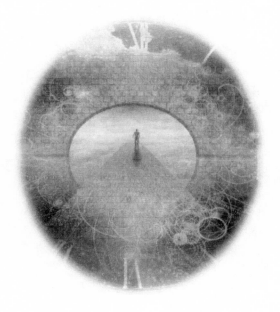

## Books by Renee Amberson

*Past Life Journeys: Time
Tripping Adventures Into Your Soul*

The ultimate guide to exploring your past lives.

*Past Lives, Future Lives: Mirrors of Time*

Travel through multidimensional vibrations
of time into and through the realms and
realities your soul has experienced.

*Magical Mind, Magical Life: How to Live a
Magical Life, Filled with Happiness and Light*

Your mind is magical. You are magical. You
hold the key to a magical life within your mind.

*Whispers Beyond the Rainbow:
Awakening Your Spiritual Self*

A magical rainbow journey inspires you
on a quest to awaken your spiritual self.

*Magical Mind Gardens: Grow Your Mind Into
a Beautiful Garden of Harmony and Joy*

Your mind is a fertile garden that will
grow whatever thoughts you plant.

*Inner Journeys: Meditations and Visualizations*

Guided visualizations can take you on many
wonderful inner journeys that lead you into the
multidimensional worlds of your mind and soul.

*Somewhere Over the Rainbow: A Soul's Journey Home*

A visionary novel about the reality of reincarnation
that offers a lighthearted look into the ups and
downs of being spiritual in a physical world.

# Echoes of Light

*Journey Into Who You Truly Are...*
*A Powerful, Spiritual Being of Light*

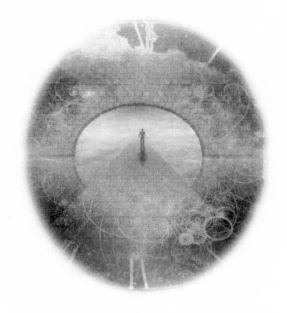

## Renee Amberson

## Light Library

# Echoes of Light

*Journey Into Who You Truly Are...*
*A Powerful, Spiritual Being of Light*

Light Library Series ~ Book Two

*Inner Journeys: Meditations and Guided Visualizations ~*
*Whispers Beyond the Rainbow: Awakening Your Spiritual Self*

© 2021 by Renee Amberson

Publisher's Cataloging-in-Publication Data

Amberson, Renee

*Echoes of Light*

1. Spirituality   2. Meditation   3. Inspiration
4. Personal Growth / Transformation   I. Title

ISBN 10: 1-883717-00-0
ISBN 13: 978-1-883717-00-1

## Light Library

https://lightlibrary.blogspot.com

This book is dedicated to your higher self...
your spiritual guide into all aspects of your life.

# Contents

⌘

## Inner Journeys

*Guided visualizations can take you on many wonderful inner journeys that lead you into the multidimensional worlds of your mind and soul.*

Inside this book you'll find metaphysical, magical, mystical meditations that will inspire and empower you on your path of self-discovery and spiritual awareness. They're offered to illuminate and guide your way as you travel an inner journey into yourself, into rediscovering your spiritual knowledge and reuniting with your higher self.

In addition, meditating offers you many practical benefits, including a refreshing, rejuvenating break from your day-to-day activities; clarity, calmness, and peace of mind; a quiet, tranquil time to tune into your inner self; a wonderful sense of relaxation and well-being; and health and harmony within your body, mind, and spirit.

## Introduction

*Inner Journeys* offers you a peaceful, quiet, tranquil time to tune into your inner self and touch your soul.

## Meditation—Inner Journeying

## The Many Ways to Meditate

Definitions and descriptions of various methods of meditation.

**Hidden Horizons** ................. 61

As you walk along the beach, you gaze out to the horizon, wondering what is beyond your line of vision.

**Canvas of Creation** ................. 63

You're in an artist's studio where there are many colors of paints, brushes, and blank canvasses for you to create all the experiences you'd like to have in your life.

**Babbling Brook** ................. 65

This stream of water has many magical things to say to you and many wonderful things to show you.

**Cushiony Clouds** ................. 67

Be inside a puffy white cloud in the sky; sink into its cushiony softness as you float leisurely along, free and light.

**Special Swan** ................. 71

Fly into the magical realms of your dreams and discover how to make all your dreams come true.

**Secluded Serenity** ................. 73

Be in a secluded cove by a quiet, calm pool of water. Feel the tranquility nurture your mind as it nourishes your soul.

**Reflections** ................. 75

Follow a sparkling stream of water in the center of a lush, beautiful valley to see where the path leads you.

**Key to Knowledge** ................. 79

In a huge hallway, you see a door, illuminated with an aura of light, that is waiting for you to open it. Somewhere inside your mind, you find a magical key that unlocks all the doors to your awareness, showing you the magic and power of your mind.

**Little Lost Leaf** ................. 81

Walking on a beautiful autumn day, you notice a vibrant, colorful leaf that has lost its connection to the tree.

Enjoy a beautiful Spring morning as the world wakes up and renews itself. Feel your own reawakening and rejuvenation as you see your spiritual growth opening up and blossoming.

Take a nature trek through a tropical rain forest where you search for and find what you are seeking.

Tune into the rhythm of the tide and the motion of harmony as you experience perfect contentment and peace all around you and within you.

## Part Two. Magical Meditations

Listen to the music inside your mind as it lightly vibrates into your thoughts and feelings, plays gently through your heart, and softly sings into your soul.

Be in a peaceful garden with lush, green plants and beautiful flowers that vibrate with health and harmony as you create perfect health, balance, and harmony of your body, mind, and spirit.

Go inside the wonderful world of your imagination and find your inner child that you left behind a long time ago.

Enjoy a gentle rainfall on a warm, summer day. Be free as a child, running joyfully through the rain.

Look inside your heart for your most treasured hope or desire. Make a wish upon a star and watch it magically appear in your world.

You receive an anonymous gift, a tapestry woven with many colorful images showing an intricate design and pattern.

**Magical Mist** ................ 115

Walking in an early morning mist, you discover a magical essence filled with a luminous light.

**Spiritual Sun Ray** ................ 117

Explore and experience a magical sun ray. Become aware of your essence and see the light of your soul reflected on the earth.

**Guardian Angel** ................ 121

See the special friend who has been with you all your life. Notice the times he or she has appeared in your life and the many ways your angel has helped, guided, and protected you.

**Healing Nourishment** ................ 125

Experience healing and renewal as you enjoy a special healing rain which nourishes and blesses you with abundant health in body, mind, and spirit.

**Releasing a Request** ................ 127

You have a very special request, a hope you'd like to see realized or a dream you'd like to have come true.

**Walking Through the Woods** ................ 129

Journey into a special forest and listen to the wisdom of a tree that shares the secrets of the earth and the universe.

**Travels of Time** ................ 133

Somewhere in your inner journeys, you meet an old spiritual master who shares a few secrets and surprises with you.

**Waterfall of Light** ................ 135

A shimmering, sparkling waterfall of light invites you to bathe in its healing energies, refreshing and rejuvenating you in body, mind, and spirit.

**Multidimensional Meadow** ................ 139

In a multidimensional meadow, filled with flowers dancing in a gentle breeze, you find you can magically commune with nature and discover beings of light who share the essence of light and shower you with joy.

Dance among the stars, weaving threads of ethereal light and universal energies into your experiences.

Ride a moonbeam into the universe and explore the infinite reaches of your mind.

## Part Three. Mystical Meditations

Gather around an old storyteller in a park and listen to the stories he tells you.

You're given a gift from the gods, a treasure more priceless and valuable than any other the physical world has to offer.

In a sacred place somewhere inside your soul, you remember who you really are—a powerful, spiritual being of light.

Watch the birth of a butterfly as it begins to emerge from its golden chrysalis; see through physical boundaries into the unlimited potential of your soul as you open your wings to fly and expand your awareness into your spiritual essence.

Ascend into the universe, traveling the steps to spirituality that lead you into your soul's evolvement and enlightenment.

In what appears to be a dream, a metaphysical master gives you a small yellow rosebud that is just beginning to open up.

Be within a whirling beam of white light to balance and blend your physical and spiritual energies with universal energy.

**Special Star** ................... 171

Travel the light of a very special star to its source in the infinite universe, to see the beginnings and the birth of this star, and the birth of your soul.

**Bridge of Light** .................. 175

Travel a bridge of light between the earth and the universe—between the physical and spiritual worlds—as you blend your inner and outer worlds together.

**Rainbow Path** .................. 179

Travel a more-than-magical journey through a shimmering rainbow in the sky to find spiritual gifts and treasures within the vibrations of each color.

**Light Library** .................. 187

Visit a library of light and read a special book about the adventures of your soul. Watch as the words come to life and portray your experiences.

**Realms of Reality** .................. 191

From somewhere in another reality, an image, a dream, or a memory appears.

**Revolving Earth** ................... 193

Journey through the infinite reaches of time to experience and explore places you've lived before in past lives, and to see your soul in an expansive, luminous vibration of light.

**Elevator to Awareness** ................... 201

A magical elevator takes you on an inner journey through time and space as it transports you into the awareness of all the experiences of your soul.

**Universal Peace Project** .................. 205

Find peace within yourself, then join a group of like-minded people and light-beings to share vibrations of love, peace, joy, and harmony throughout the world and the universe.

**Mystical Moonlight** ................... 207

Explore the effervescent energy of moonlight reflecting on a still, quiet pool of water as you simultaneously experience the light shimmering from the universe and sparkling from within your soul, vibrating in harmony.

Take a brief journey "home" to experience the essence of your soul.

Travel into and beyond the center of the sunrise and experience the dawning of the light within you.

The inner journey continues...

*A magical rainbow journey inspires you on a quest to awaken your spiritual self.*

Listen to the whispers from your soul reminding you of the true nature of your spirit. Follow a rainbow path inside a dream as you explore a light library  to read a book that's all about your soul, attend classes at the school of spirituality in the universe, travel a majestic mountain to find gifts from your spiritual self, discover a music box that plays the symphony of the stars, dance with the spirits of dawn as you journey into the center of a sunrise, travel a rainbow bridge into seven soul gardens, and experience a healing waterfall of light as you journey to awakening your spiritual self.

As you continue on your rainbow path within, you'll watch the birth of a butterfly as it begins to emerge from its golden chrysalis as you see through physical boundaries into the knowledge of your soul as you open your wings to fly and expand your awareness into your spiritual essence.

The light of your soul shimmers like iridescent butterfly wings. **Whispers** is a visionary novella, written as a meditation that invites you to travel on the wings of your spirit to explore the multidimensional realms within you and the worlds of the universe around you to remember who you truly are... a powerful, spiritual being of light.

A magical rainbow journey invites you to look for the light within yourself and reawaken your spiritual self.

### Part One. Whispers

## Part Two. Shimmers

## Part Three. Soul Gardens

## About the Author

# Inner
# Journeys

# Introduction

⸙

The meditations inside this book originated from special journeys in my mind, secret places in my heart, and sacred spaces in my soul. They've all spoken to me in a meaningful way and I'd like to share them with you.

I hope you'll enjoy them as much or more than I have, and that they'll bring you many inner experiences of joy and harmony as you blend your inner world with your outer experiences. I hope they'll encourage and empower you on your path of self-discovery and aid you in remembering your spiritual knowledge and reawakening to your true spiritual self.

It is also my sincere hope that the meditations in this book—in addition to being soothing and relaxing, and in some cases quite energizing—will help you open up your inner knowing to attain a higher level of awareness and insight, and will show you the spiritual symbolism and the magic in your everyday activities and experiences.

There are many forms of meditation and meditation takes many forms. This book offers you inner journeys in the form of guided visualizations—imageries for your body, mind, and spirit. Inside this book, you'll find meditations that will open your heart and mind, empower you to tune into your inner self, and grow your soul into the awareness of the spiritual light-being that you truly are.

*Inner Journeys* offers you a peaceful, quiet, tranquil time to tune into your inner self and touch your soul. The meditations show you how to remember, rediscover, and reawaken to your soul's natural vibration of love, peace, joy, and harmony as they invite you to journey into special places in your mind, secret places within your heart, and sacred spaces inside your soul to show you the many joys and wonders and treasures you have within you.

The meditations invite you to re-open the inner world of your soul's knowledge to remind you of your spiritual nature, and show you the way inside the words to the images in your mind—to travel a mystical journey into the awareness of your soul.

As you journey inside your mind with the images drawn from words, you'll be opening and experiencing many wonderful worlds within yourself and exploring mystical mindscapes in a very special place within your soul.

There are three types of meditation presented in this book. The first type is unguided meditation—simply relaxing and entering a quiet, still, peaceful place in your mind. This offers you several options—to think about nothing at all, to just relax and refresh yourself, to center and focus yourself in the present moment, or to calm your conscious mind to relieve stress.

To enter and be in an unguided meditation, simply focus your attention and awareness on your breathing to relax you as you simultaneously calm and quiet your conscious mind. To open and experience the images inside your mind to see where they'll take you and what they'll show you, just relax and let it happen; go with the flow. Let go of any preconceived ideas or feelings; open your mind to receive your awareness from within. Your inner imagery and insights will show you what you need to see.

Another way to experience this is to open the book at random, read the meditation on that page, and go with the flow. Allow the meditation you've chosen, seemingly by chance, to resonate within you. You'll find that your intuition has opened to the page that holds the answer to a question you may have, or a solution to a problem you might be puzzling over.

Maybe the meditation will provide you with information you need to know, or show you something that will be helpful or beneficial to you in some area of your life. It may address a particular concern you might have, or it may spark an idea or insight that offers you what you most need at the moment.

The second type is self-guided, where you meditate on whatever you choose. You originate and create the images; you design and direct your own meditation. You can explore and experience anything you want; you can go wherever you choose in your mind, and you can achieve any purpose you desire. This is a wonderful way to access your intuition and inner knowing, and to open up and expand the power of your mind.

The third type is guided visualization, which leads you in a definite direction and is intended to achieve specific results. The meditations and visualizations in this book are worded to be interactive, and are either gently guided or provide you with the beginnings of a self-guided meditation. They offer you images and suggestions to get you started, then your mind will take over to guide you and show you what is within.

Whatever you experience in your meditations will be filtered and colored by your frame of reference. You're a unique, special individual and your mind will offer you the images and insights that are most meaningful and appropriate for you.

While I've worded the meditations in an open way for you to experience and explore whatever comes into your mind in a unique and individual manner, and to interpret what you experience in your own way, several of them are designed to guide you in a specific direction and to achieve certain purposes, such as for healing or meeting your guardian angel.

Some of the meditations are short, offering a few descriptive paragraphs that provide the essence of the intended imagery or they present several ideas and suggestions with general instructions that will inspire you to image and create your inner journey for yourself.

Rely on your mind to give you the images, thoughts, and feelings that will guide your self-exploration and discoveries. This is a powerful way to open your imagination and see inside your inner knowing. In this way, the words come to life, inviting you on an inner journey where the words flow like a magical stream of water and show you a place where inner images bloom.

The words in the meditation will begin to inspire and draw images in your mind, and open into thoughts and feelings, then you will take it from there, guided by your own inner imagery and by where your subconscious mind—your inner, spiritual self—takes you.

As you may notice in some of the meditations, the teacher in me slips out from time to time. This is most apparent in the suggestions and notes I offer after a few of the meditations. Please accept these as other avenues to explore, if you choose, as you open windows and doorways on your own.

I'd like to think you will allow the meditations in this book to shine a light on your journeys that will be helpful to you in finding and illuminating the truth for yourself. Your true teacher is within, and you find your own truth by looking within yourself and discovering what is real for you by following your feelings.

Your mind is waiting to show you many magical and mystical worlds within yourself. Set aside some time just for you—a special, spiritual time for yourself—to relax and tune into who you really are, to touch your inner essence and feel the shimmers of your soul resonating within you.

By taking a few moments every day, or every now and then, to meditate, you'll see and feel the light of your soul reflected within you and mirrored all around you, as your soul-light brightens, expands, and radiates out into the world.

Let your mind be your guide through the wonderful world of your inner images, through the worlds of your insights and inner awareness. Enjoy the meditations, guided visualizations, and self-guided imageries in this book. Allow them to inspire you to explore many other areas of awareness within yourself as you reach into, through, and above your mind into deeper dimensions of your true spiritual self.

# Meditation

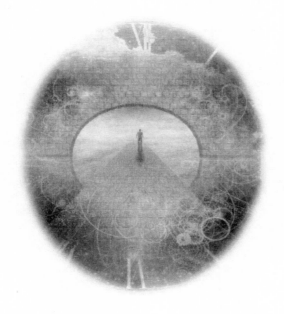

## *Inner Journeying*

# The Many Ways to Meditate

*Definitions and descriptions of
various methods of meditation.*

There are many ways to meditate and many methods of meditation. You've probably practiced some of these in one way or another. All forms of meditation are wonderful and have two things in common: physical relaxation and focusing your complete attention and awareness into your subconscious mind.

Meditation takes on many forms and expressions. Meditation can be so much more than sitting quietly or chanting. Meditation provides a direct pathway into your subconscious mind—into the knowing awareness you have within yourself.

Meditation can range anywhere from lightly exploring your imagination to deeply experiencing your awareness. The following list is not comprehensive or all-inclusive; it briefly describes various ways to meditate and offers some metaphysical uses and everyday applications of meditation.

### Active

Taking long, peaceful walks through the woods or along the beach, or in another natural setting where you feel comfortable and at ease, allows you to tune into nature and to be at one with the world around you and in touch with the world within you, with the naturalness of yourself.

Being in nature—in a beautiful, natural place—replenishes and rejuvenates you, and has a wonderful calming effect on both your body and your mind. This is because nature is in harmony with itself and inspires that same feeling within you.

### Breathing

Breathing in and out, slowly and deeply—peacefully and purposely—as you take a moment or two for yourself provides a change of mind and focus of awareness. Focusing completely on your breathing allows you to calm your thoughts and center into yourself.

### Chanting

Slowly repeating a specific syllable or word, usually the word "OM" (pronounced ohm) or "HU" (pronounced hue) helps you clear and calm your conscious mind. The vibration of the word focuses your mind and centers your attention within yourself. It also helps to put you in touch with a higher power, with the essence of your spiritual self.

### Guided Imagery

The imagery of words draws pictures and creates scenes in your mind as the meditation guides you into a gentle feeling of peaceful relaxation for quiet contemplation, reflection, and/or the enjoyment of going within your subconscious mind to open up and explore whatever the words inspire as they lead you into wherever your mind and spirit take you.

Guided imagery also serves specific purposes; it can help you relieve stress, achieve goals, facilitate healing, and open the magical, mystical power of your mind.

### Mindfulness

Being completely aware of what you're doing and where you're at keeps you centered and connected with your current emotions and experiences. By focusing on your breathing and placing your full awareness and attention into yourself and your surroundings, you become present in the very real moment of here and now.

### Musings

To muse about something is to pay full attention to it, to ponder it deeply, and to let it flow, gently and easily on your mind to gather more information. Musing could also be considered a synonym for meditation.

Many creative people, such as writers, artists, and musicians often listen to the muse in their mind to receive inspiration for their creative endeavors.

### Prayer

Directing your attention toward a divine essence, being, or higher power that you perceive to be outside of yourself, such as the Universe, God, Buddha, or an angel or spiritual guide, can help you focus your desires, thoughts, and feelings. It is most often used as a channel for requests or to receive answers, insights, and assistance from higher sources. Prayer helps to put you in touch with your divine, inner spiritual essence, and serves the purpose of guiding you within to your own higher power.

### Relaxation

Simply sitting in a comfortable chair to relax or stretching out on a couch to quietly think your thoughts, or to just breathe and be, is a wonderful form of meditation. Relaxation is actually the first step to meditating. As your body relaxes, and your conscious mind becomes calm and quiet, you free yourself from all the cares and worries of the day as you naturally tune into your inner peaceful essence.

### Reveries

Thinking, imagining, creating, and seeing various situations and scenarios happening in your mind allows you to explore your inner feelings. Similar to unguided visualizations and daydreams, where your mind wanders into other realms of reality, reveries allow your mind to meander through the myriad paths that your feelings take you on as your imagination shows you the different possible and probable ways your experiences could play out.

Reveries offer you the opportunity to quietly think about and ponder your thoughts, to open your insights, ideas, and intuition, to reflect on past experiences, to look into and explore present events more deeply, or to contemplate future plans, dreams, and goals.

Reveries are sometimes used to help counteract boredom by empty-mindedly gazing out the window, or zoning out during a dull lecture or business meeting, or imagining yourself in another place doing something enjoyable.

While getting "lost" in a mindless place or changing your perceptual awareness by going somewhere else more appealing in your thoughts serves a purpose by allowing you to escape reality for a few moments, reveries do much more than that. They offer you insightful and intuitive mind trips.

By analyzing and interpreting their content, they very often—sometimes literally and sometimes symbolically—give you answers to something you've been considering or wondering about and puzzling over. At times, they simply offer your conscious mind a much-needed respite from stress or anxiety.

### Shamanic Journeying

Traveling into and through non-ordinary realities is used primarily to journey into the higher and lower worlds for physical and spiritual healing, as well as to enter astral and ethereal realms for insight and spiritual knowledge.

Shamans journey through time and space to visit other realities for many other purposes, such as soul retrieval and to speak with another person's heart, or to connect with past or future selves or events to see and recreate the past in a new way, or to design and alter the future.

Shamans often connect with the spirits of nature and call upon their power animals and other allies and spiritual entities to request their protection and assistance, or to guide them in achieving whatever they are doing. This is usually accompanied by drumming and chanting, dancing and ritual.

Many people use quiet meditation or imagery to achieve the same thing; to enter an altered state of consciousness to access their natural, inborn healing abilities, and to be more in tune with their spiritual essence. Many times we go on shamanic journeys in our dreams and astral projections.

### Transcendental

Elevating your mind above the mundane, physical world allows you to detach your consciousness and your emotions from cares and worries, raising your awareness to a higher plane as you let go of conscious, trivial thoughts and feelings. The mind is perfectly calm, centered, and tranquil, bringing a deep, relaxing feeling of peace.

### Visualization

Visualization is seeing with your mind's eye, using imagery to clearly visualize yourself doing or achieving something first in your mind to help you manifest it in your life. An example is athletes who use visualization to see themselves excelling in their sports by focusing their awareness and picturing the way a certain event will happen to help them achieve their desired result.

Another example is visualizing a tangible, touchable goal to help you attain it, such as buying a house or a new car. Using imagery to clearly see, feel, and experience something in your mind as if it is real, as if it is actually happening, allows you to fully experience it and to manifest it on a physical level. Visualization also has tremendous value and benefit in healing, and can bring about seemingly "miraculous" cures.

Visualization is similar to mind projection, where you project your awareness into a past, present, or future scene to help you clearly understand it, or to create it in the way you desire. When used for manifesting, it is always a good idea to keep the thought in mind that whatever you desire will happen for the highest good of all involved.

You unconsciously use visualization, and your feelings and thought energy, every day in every moment and experience to create your reality. Conscious visualization allows you to be more focused and aware of what you're doing.

### Yoga and T'ai Chi

These forms of meditation consist of slow, gentle stretches and body postures, combined with rhythmic breathing and conscious awareness of your body, mind, and spirit working together as a unified whole. The exercises and movements harmonize body and mind, and balance both the physical and spiritual flow of energy within your body. They focus your awareness, allowing you to achieve centered calmness and clarity of mind. These and other forms of Eastern exercise and philosophy are also referred to as meditation in motion.

### Zen

Meditating on nothing or emptiness by completely clearing and stilling your conscious mind is referred to as sitting. You focus your attention on your breathing to bring you inner peace and stillness of mind.

If a conscious thought enters your awareness while you are meditating and attempts to interrupt you, you acknowledge it as merely a thought and gently let it go, without attaching any feelings to it or giving it any importance, or thinking about or dwelling on it. You simply allow your mind to be quiet. This can be very calming, relaxing, and peaceful, as well as spiritually nourishing and rejuvenating in stressful times.

Another form of Zen meditation is known as mindful meditation, where you focus completing on what you are doing and what is happening in the present moment of here and now.

There are many ways to meditate and many ways to use meditation. One way is not better than another; they're simply different from each other. Many of the forms are similar and tend to meld together, merging into aspects of one another.

You can meditate using some combination of all of the above at various times, depending on your individual desires, needs, preferences, lifestyle, and circumstances.

Just go with the flow. Whatever works for you that brings you feelings of peacefulness and a calm mind, and helps you incorporate meditation into your daily life, is the best way for you to meditate.

# Principles and Purposes

⟨∾⟩

*Value and benefits of meditation.*
*Practical and metaphysical applications.*

The many physical and spiritual values and benefits of meditating are far-reaching and multi-faceted. Meditation can help you in any area of your life you desire. The manner and many various ways in which you can use it are unlimited.

The first step to meditating—to getting inside your subconscious mind—is just simply relaxing; this automatically and naturally promotes health and harmony in body, mind, and spirit. The holistic value of meditation and its effect on mind-body connections is intricately interrelated. When you use self-guided imagery or a guided visualization in an aware, focused, and directed manner, you greatly expand and enhance your body's own natural ability to heal itself.

Meditation is wonderfully uplifting. It can bring your spirits up, and change your mood and perceptions if you're feeling sad or depressed, discouraged or worried. It's a great way to take care of the blahs and is a super five-minute refresher that rejuvenates you and improves your attitude.

Meditating can help you recognize deep and powerful emotions that may be affecting you unconsciously, and to bring them into your conscious mind. It offers a gentle, nurturing way to look into negative and/or traumatic feelings and memories. It helps you get in touch with, tune into, and understand your true feelings.

Meditation is self-empowering. It allows you to go within yourself to reclaim your personal power to achieve self-growth and to make clear, conscious choices and changes in your life that will help you move in a positive direction.

Meditating helps you become more aware of your inner self and to recognize and reunite with your spiritual self. It opens a window to your inner knowing and your awareness of your true nature; it helps you remember and rediscover your spiritual knowledge by inviting you to visit sacred spaces in your soul.

Meditation offers you spiritual enlightenment. You can use meditation to explore multidimensional realms within your mind to give you insights and perspectives that can provide you with alternative avenues of perception to clearly see into and understand the spiritual symbolism of your experiences, and to really know what's inside your soul.

# Rhythm of Relaxing

—————————— ✂ ——————————

*Relax your body and calm your conscious mind as*
*you open your subconscious and spiritual awareness.*

There's an art to meditating—to getting inside your subconscious mind to that still, quiet, peaceful place within you, to that spiritual realm of knowing awareness where you can reconnect with your inner self and reawaken to your true essence—and it's easy to do.

All you have to do is breathe naturally, relax your body as you calm your conscious mind, and allow images to form inside the wonderful world of your imagination and inner knowing. As your conscious mind becomes calm and quiet, and your body becomes relaxed, you tune out the physical world for a time as you tune into a meditative, more aware frame of mind.

Find a quiet time during the day or evening, and a place where you can be alone. Let yourself relax before you read and experience a meditation. Breathe in some nice, deep, relaxing, cleansing breaths and let them out slowly, feeling your body begin to relax. Let go of any stresses and negativity. Let all the tension ease out of your body.

Let go of your conscious thoughts and cares; let them just drift away. Let yourself feel peaceful, calm, and quiet within yourself. Let your breathing relax you. As you're breathing in and out, slowly and naturally, allow a soft, easy, soothing, peaceful feeling of relaxation flow deeply down into and through every part of your body, relaxing you completely.

Imagine this feeling and your breathing as a very gentle wave of motion that flows softly into and through you, descending gradually and slowly from the top of your head all the way through the tips of your toes, feeling the gentle, harmonious feelings of relaxation circulate softly through your body.

Allow your mind to become quiet, open, and receptive to the many beautiful and wonderful imageries, thoughts, sensations, feelings, and emotions you will become aware of and experience as you meditate.

Taking a moment or two to meditate—to allow yourself to relax, to calmly breathe and to just "be" when you're feeling stressed out or overwhelmed—is a special gift you give yourself. This can uplift you into a refreshing place of peace and calm, and offers a rejuvenating break from your day-to-day activities and responsibilities. A few quiet moments of meditation bring you clarity and peace of mind, as well as a wonderful sense of relaxation and well-being.

# Learning the Language of Your Mind

*Stretch your mind and your imagination as you
see and sense how your subconscious speaks to you.*

Your subconscious mind communicates with you through the imagery of words. It speaks to you by showing you symbols and imagery, and talks to you through your thoughts and feelings, using pictures instead of words; it's the language of your mind. The thoughts you hear, the feelings you sense, and the pictures you see in your mind originate in your imagination—the world of your inner images.

The following mind-opening meditation is a self-guided visualization that will help you gently stretch your mind and open your imagination as you learn the language of your mind. Take your time inside your mind—inside your imagination—to completely explore, experience, and enjoy every part of this meditation.

Before you begin, think about this analogy for a few minutes. Your subconscious mind—your inner awareness—is like a bud that's growing into a very beautiful flower. Allow it to grow at its own rate. Nurture it with care and loving attention. As a bud, it needs time to develop and open up, to flower and bloom, and to flourish and grow into a beautiful garden.

Start your meditation by relaxing and breathing. Enter into a calm, peaceful, quiet place within you. Ease and erase the tension and tightness from your body. Clear your thoughts and feelings of your everyday experiences and open yourself up to experiencing the magic inside your mind.

Imagine and create a yellow rosebud in your mind. Take your time; be very descriptive and detailed in your visualization. Feel and sense this rosebud with every part of your mind and your imagination. Use all your physical senses in an inner way to see, hear, smell, touch, and taste the vibrations and energies of this beautiful yellow rosebud. Breathe in and be the essence of the rosebud inside you.

As you imagine and create the rosebud, clearly visualize the image; see the thought of it in your mind. The thought itself will draw a picture for you. Perhaps this meditation will inspire a memory of when you saw a beautiful yellow rosebud, or another image, thought, or feeling will appear in your mind, or you may just get a sense of the rosebud.

Maybe you'll remember when someone sent you roses and what they looked and smelled like, and what they felt like as you gently touched the petals, or you'll remember when you had a single rose in a vase in your home or on your desk at work. Perhaps you'll recall the last time you saw and smelled a rose when you were outside, and you'll also become aware of what the weather was like and all the many other sights and sounds around you.

Perhaps the meditation will bring forth an image of a rosebush in your own garden that is beginning to bud and open up. As you meditate on what you see, sense, and feel, the image will begin to move, to flow with the momentum of your meditation. Perhaps you'll see a scene with several images that move and change as you become more involved with and aware of them.

Your subconscious shows you images of your thoughts and feelings. Open yourself up to completely experiencing—with all your physical and inner senses, with every part of your mind and your imagination, and on all levels of your awareness—what your subconscious shows you.

By accepting the pictures your mind offers you, you open a channel of communication between your conscious and subconscious mind. Much like your dream images which are offered to you every night, the images you see in your meditations—the thoughts, ideas, and insights you become aware of and the feelings you experience—will be meaningful for you in a very special way. Be open and receptive to even the smallest details and intricacies, as these hold valuable information and knowledge for you. Just go with the flow to see what your subconscious shows you and what it has to say to you.

When you're done with this meditation, and while everything you experienced is clear and vivid in your mind, take some time to quietly think about and to reflect on the images you saw, the thoughts you heard, and the feelings you became aware of.

This quiet time after a meditation allows you to bring your inner knowing and subconscious awareness into your conscious mind, where you can fully understand it on all levels of your awareness. This quiet time to flow the images and insights into your conscious mind also allows you to bring more of what you experienced on your inner journey into your conscious awareness.

You might want to write down what you saw and felt. Completely describe the images you saw in your mind, the thoughts you became aware of, and the feelings they brought forth. Define what they represent to you on an inner, feeling level. This helps you remember more of your meditation, understand it better, and incorporate it into your physical consciousness.

It's also helpful to completely immerse yourself in your meditations, to focus your full attention on them, and to go inside each image and feeling to see what your subconscious is showing you and saying to you. Become totally involved with your imagination to feel or sense what your images are really like, and what they represent to you. This helps you understand the language of your mind and will also help you open up your imagination and develop your intuition. Note any thoughts, ideas, or insights that come to you when you're in a meditative frame of mind—a level of increased awareness.

At first you may think you're making up what you experience, that you're playing with your imagination. This isn't true. What you're really doing is opening up your inner imagery and spiritual knowing, to see the truth within you. You're setting your subconscious mind free to show you what you already know. Learn to trust your feelings and what comes into your mind as a genuine reflection of your inner knowing by accepting whatever you experience as real and true.

To understand the thoughts and feelings you become aware of, and the insights you receive, or the imagery you see and sense, and what they represent to you, ask your subconscious—your inner self—for the interpretations and answers. Let this inner knowing come softly into your conscious mind. Ponder the images and thoughts a bit; let them be gentle on your mind. By doing this, you'll open your inner awareness even more, you'll gain a better understanding of what your subconscious is saying to you, and a clearer understanding of what it is showing you.

Meditating helps you open your intuition and imagination, to enter and explore the magical world of your inner images and spiritual knowing, to reconnect with your inner self and reunite with your spiritual self—the one who speaks to you through your thoughts, ideas, images, insights, and feelings—the one who whispers to you in your mind.

Your imagination is where you rediscover the real you, where you're totally free to be who you really are. It's where you find that very special, sacred part of you that is within every area of your life from the blah to the blissful.

When you tune into this special place within yourself, you also bring your inner, more perceptive awareness into your physical experiences where you can see the reflections of your true spiritual nature mirrored in all your everyday activities and experiences as you blend your inner knowing into both your conscious and subconscious worlds simultaneously.

Your images, intuition, insights, and imagination will teach you the language of your mind and show you your inner knowing. Your true teacher is within. Listen to yourself.

# Peaceful Place

❧

*Create a peaceful place within your mind
where you experience perfect harmony and
feel the joy of just being who you really are.*

An important part of meditation is having a peaceful place inside your mind. It's like a "home base" or a retreat, and is an inner sanctuary.

Imagine and create a very special place in your mind that's all your own. See and sense a beautiful scene—a quiet, tranquil place, where you enjoy being peaceful, calm, and happy within yourself. Envision a place where you feel completely comfortable and natural, where you can connect with yourself and truly be who you really are.

Your peaceful place is a magical place where you can open up the complete awareness of your mind, where you can tune into your inner self and listen to your inner voice. It's a place where you can experience perfect peace and total harmony within yourself.

Your peaceful place might be a place in nature. It might be a private beach, where you listen to the sound of the waves as they gently ebb and flow, and watch them as they softly touch the shore.

It might be a walking path in a forest, where you hear the wind gently moving through the leaves in the trees, whispering to you, or perhaps a clearing in the woods with shafts of hazy sunlight filtering through the treetops and playing with patterns on the forest floor, or perhaps it is a completely open area with sunlight streaming in.

Your peaceful place might be a wide-open, grassy meadow with wildflowers growing free, where you view the horizon clearly in all directions and you feel as free and light as the breeze. It might be a garden with beautiful, fragrant flowers that radiate health and harmony. It might be a mountain rising majestically into the sky, or a lush, green valley, surrounded by trees.

It might be a calm, placid lake or a gently-rippling brook with large stones you walk across. It might be a clear, sparkling stream of water, or a quiet pond that reflects the sky and the sun. It might be a secluded cove with clear, green-blue water and lush, flowering bushes, or a magnificent waterfall cascading down over shimmering rocks.

It might be a special place of being-ness, an atmosphere of knowing inside your mind, with its own aura and ambiance, or a sanctuary of spiritual awareness within a multidimensional realm. Your peaceful place might be an entirely new place that you create entirely with your imagination, or a place that you remember and re-create from a dream or a distant memory. Your peaceful place is wherever and whatever you want it to be.

Take your time with this self-guided meditation to think about the kind of place you'd like to have as your peaceful place. Give your thoughts, images, and feelings a lot of careful consideration. Pay special attention to your feelings to know how you really feel about the scene you're seeing, imagining, and creating.

Then close your eyes and create a detailed and colorful picture of that scene in your mind. Be very descriptive; become totally involved with creating your peaceful place. See it clearly in your mind's eye and get a strong sense or feeling about it. As you begin to imagine and create it, to see it and sense it, a few images or a full-blown picture may appear in your mind.

You might see an exact replica of your thoughts or your mind may surprise you with an entirely different scene than what you had envisioned, with images created from your feelings in a magical place inside your mind. Whatever you see and create, and/or re-create, is the most perfect peaceful place for you.

After you've created your peaceful place, go inside your images; be totally there in your peaceful place. Completely sense and experience it with every part of you—with every part of your awareness. Really notice how you feel when you're there; notice the atmosphere and the ambiance. Take some time for yourself—all the time you want—to be inside your inner, magical world of meditation.

Come to this place often and for any reason. Aside from the obvious benefits of being able to go into your peaceful place at any time to be calm and tranquil, to just relax for a few moments, to let go of stress and tension that may build up during your day, or to turn the blahs into the blissful, you can come here to refresh, replenish, and revitalize your body and your mind—to heal, nourish, and rejuvenate your inner spirit.

It's a wonderful, private place to just be you, to get back in touch with yourself and be who you really are in a carefree, joyous state of mind. It's a place where you can hear yourself think, a place to meditate. It's a place to feel peace and harmony within yourself, a place to just breathe and BE.

# Part One

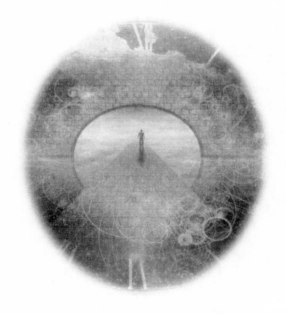

*Metaphysical Meditations*

**Part One** centers on the theme of
self-discovery and spiritual awareness, of
exploring the harmony of your body, mind, and
spirit, and how they're intricately intertwined.

Inside this part, you'll find metaphysical
meditations and visualizations to soothe and
heal your body, to revitalize and energize
you, to open up and expand your mind, and
to soar into your spirit. They share with you
the secrets of your soul, if you will listen to
the soft, quiet voice that whispers within.

These meditations invite you into the center of
yourself, to see your spiritual self reflected in all
your thoughts, feelings, and experiences, and in
every part of your everyday activities. They offer
you a way to blend your physical consciousness
with your spiritual awareness, and to be at one
with the world around you and within you.

They hold the promise of opening up your inner
knowing, as they show you the natural power of
your mind and reveal your true spiritual nature,
if you will look within yourself to see the images
in your imagination—to remember, rediscover,
and recognize how special and real they are.

# Glorious Gondola

*Board a beautiful boat and travel through
the magical, mystical waterways in your mind.*

Imagine you're boarding a beautiful boat, an ornate and glorious gondola, as you begin to travel a magical path—a mystical waterway through your imagination that leads you into your mind and soul—into your spiritual awareness.

The oarsman is a most knowledgeable guide, having traveled this way many times before, who will lead you safely and serenely through all the avenues and waterways in this magical, mystical place—your mind.

As you travel your inner journeys through the images, thoughts, and feelings inside you, inside the many multidimensional realms and realities of your soul, and the wonderful worlds of your inner knowing within you, you'll begin to remember and recognize your inherent spiritual symbols.

The world of your inner images—your imagination—shows itself easily through pictures that represent various aspects of your mind and soul. Some of these symbols are universal, shared by all, but most of them are unique and special to you, and are based on your beliefs and frame of reference.

The symbols you see may change from time to time, depending on your understanding and interpretation, and on your level of awareness, perception, and insight. The images you see in your mind may also show themselves differently with your current mood, experiences, thoughts, and feelings.

In this visualization, the waterway represents your subconscious mind and the oarsman (guide) is your inner, spiritual self that you may already be aware of or will begin to recognize and remember as you travel the inner journeys in and through your heart, mind, and soul. The boat represents your imagination, the vehicle through which you travel.

Allow your inner self to guide you knowledgeably through all the metaphysical, magical, and mystical paths and places in your mind and heart, through the sometimes hidden and sacred spaces in your soul, and to gently guide you through all the experiences in your life, whether they be inner journeys or outer experiences.

In this self-guided meditation, imagine you're boarding a boat that can take you anywhere you want to go and for any reason you want to go there. See what your mind has to show you and what your soul has to share with you.

Bon voyage!

# Splendor of the Sunset

⤸

*Experience the majesty of a sunset; see the vibrant
colors and hues reflected on the clouds and mirrored
within your mind, illuminating the essence of your soul.*

It's a warm, pleasant evening and you're out for a quiet stroll, just enjoying the gentle breeze and the subdued, calm feel of the early twilight. As you gaze up toward the horizon and the sky above you, your attention and awareness is completely caught and absorbed in the sunset.

You see numerous billowy, multicolored clouds etched with layers of radiant mauve combining into varying degrees and shades of orange, ranging from a bright, brilliant orange graduating into tones of peach blending into a pearl-ish pink that is coalescing and variegating into coral, uniting with hues of rose and highlights of dusky violet mixed with both azure and dusty blue intermingling with nuances of powder gray interspersed on the clouds higher above the horizon, reflecting the beauty and magnificence of the sun's splendor of rays splashed across the twilight sky.

The sky is filled with the most beautiful sunset you've ever seen—the most beautiful sunset in the world. As you experience the awe and wonder, and the majesty and splendor of this ever-changing sunset, you feel the colors within and through every part of you, filling you as you share the sunset with the sky.

As you become the sunset, as you breathe in and become one with the essence of the sunset, at one with the essence of twilight that is simultaneously radiant and vibrant, calm and gentle, you blend your awareness with the splendor and subdued energies of the colors illuminating the sky. The warm, soft breeze gently circles around you, sharing the colors and the quiet feel of early twilight with the earth and the universe as the colors and feelings emanate into and through your spiritual awareness and essence.

As the sun begins to slowly dip and disappear under the horizon, you see the rays of gloriously radiant and vibrant orange and purple hues on the line of the horizon reflected on the bottom of the clouds and mirrored within your mind as they simultaneously ground you to the earth and allow your spirit to soar into the universe.

Breathe in and be the beauty and harmony and splendor of the colors and the energies of the sunset inside you, inside your mind and soul. Feel the vibrations of the colors radiate and expand inside you, flowing outward to the earth and the universe, showing you the many wondrous hues and tones of the colors, and the essence and many expressions of your soul.

# Sounds of the Seashore

*Sit by the ocean and listen to the ebb and flow of*
*the tide. Allow the sounds to just simply relax you and*
*take you into soothing, serene places within your mind.*

Imagine you're sitting in the warm sand on the beach on a beautiful summer day. You feel completely relaxed; you're totally enjoying the sights and sounds of the seashore, and this perfect day.

Soak up the misty rays of light from the sun that are reflected from the big, puffy, white clouds that float lazily through the azure-blue sky. Watch the waves as they gently wash up on the shore. Listen to the ebb and flow of the tide. Allow the warmth of the sun and the sound of the waves as they softy splash on the sand to completely relax you and take you into soothing, serene places within your mind.

Let your thoughts and feelings drift in and out with the sound of the tide. Close your eyes and watch the images inside your mind float gently in tune with the rhythm of the ocean. Feel your mind blending in harmony with the motion of the gentle waves as they softly wash into your awareness.

Breathe in the calm breeze and smell the scent of the ocean air. Be in the pleasant warmth and gentle quiet of this beautiful, perfect day. Sense yourself—your awareness—blending completely into this soft, soothing, serene moment of here and now, feeling perfectly content and at peace with yourself.

# Wonderful Waterfall

_____ ❧ _____

*Explore and experience the power and
exhilaration of a wonderful waterfall
cascading down a beautiful mountainside.*

It's a pleasantly warm summer day and you're outside exploring and enjoying the natural wonders and beauties of the earth. You've been hiking for several miles along the base of a softly-sloping mountain when you hear the sound of a waterfall.

Listening to determine the direction, you let the sound guide you toward the tall bushes and large rocks you see just beyond the curve ahead of you. Walking that way, you begin to smell the scent of the water and you can almost see a rainbow in your mind.

Getting closer to the waterfall, the rushing, roaring sound energizes you, and you feel a wonderful power and exhilaration building inside you. Parting the bushes, you see a magnificent waterfall gushing with life as it cascades down the mountainside, splashing and shimmering off the rocks and the lush greenery that surrounds it on both sides.

Every drop of water sparkles and shimmers as it catches the sunlight and reflects beautiful rainbows everywhere as the waterfall pours into a swirling, foaming pool beneath.

You know you've discovered a very special place, an area of wonder and beauty, and you laugh with happiness and delight. Stepping through the bushes and getting closer to the waterfall, you feel the misty spray gently touch your face and envelop your body with its magical rainbow aura.

The waterfall is surging with motion. Standing there for a few moments, enjoying the sounds, scents, and sights of this very wonderful place, you watch the waterfall tumbling down the mountainside, sensing its exuberant energy within you.

The pool beneath the waterfall looks inviting. Knowing it's perfectly safe, you decide to go for a swim, so you drop your backpack and take off your shoes. Stretching in the sunlight and feeling a wonderful sense of aliveness and freedom, you dive into the water, experiencing the coolness and surging motion of the water all around you.

Surfacing, you yell with sheer joy and exuberance, completely in tune with the wonderful, powerful energies of this waterfall. The water refreshes and revitalizes you, invigorating every part of your body, mind, and spirit.

Climbing out of the pool and sitting on the rocks to dry in the warmth of the sun, you feel the powerful energy of the waterfall surging within you, knowing that when you dove into the water, you became part of it and it became part of you.

# Crystal Clarity

————————— ⅋ —————————

*Look into a clear crystal ball that radiates with a*
*vibrant glow of energy as it opens your intuition and*
*illuminates the imagery of your thoughts and feelings.*

Closing your eyes and looking inside a special place in your mind, you see a clear crystal ball that radiates with the vibrant energy of light. Looking into the crystal, you sense yourself being drawn into it—beginning to vibrate to the light and energies emanating from the crystal.

The energy seems to come from within the crystal and from within the center of your mind and your essence at the same time. You feel the energies vibrating all around you and within you, radiating out from deep inside you.

As the light and energy vibrations from the crystal—from the light and energies within you—illuminate and energize the imagery of your thoughts and feelings, you feel your mind opening up and expanding, and you begin to see the still and silent images of your thoughts and feelings as they form in your mind and start to sparkle into your awareness.

At first, they may be blurry and a bit hazy, but then they begin to vibrate into a multicolored panorama of pictures and a kaleidoscope of images that shape and shift in slow motion through your vision and in your feelings.

As you center your attention and awareness on the images you see within your mind, they become much more sharply focused, more clearly defined and descriptive, and you easily see the pictures of your thoughts and feelings. The pictures are so vivid and detailed that you wonder if you're seeing them with your physical eyes or with your mind's eye.

You open your eyes and look around at the physical things that surround you, and you realize you're seeing the images of your thoughts and feelings as clearly as you see physical objects. This seems so amazing to you, and so delightful—to see and feel the energy vibrations of your thoughts and feelings with your inner senses.

You close your eyes again and now you notice that the vibrations of the pictures, images, thoughts, and feelings you see and feel within your mind are transformed into coherent, cohesive, clear scenes—moving pictures—that you completely understand.

There is a knowing inside you that you've always been able to see and sense the vibrations of your thoughts and feelings as clearly as you see with your physical eyes and experience with your physical senses. As you realize this, the crystal begins to glow with a radiant, even more luminous vibration of energy, and you sense your energies and awareness opening up and expanding even more within your mind.

The crystal has become a glowing ball of energy, emanating a vibrant radiance and a brilliant light that gently enters into and through every part of your mind as the inner vibrations of your thoughts and feelings open up in much more detail and clarity inside you, becoming much more energized within you.

It's an incredible, wonderful, magical feeling. You know you have the power to clearly and consciously see and sense and feel and understand both the seen and unseen energy vibrations that emanate from all your thoughts and feelings.

But even more than that, you're able to see into and through anything and everything—into all the emotions and events and experiences in your life, to understand and know every part of them, and to see the expressions of your thoughts and feelings from the inside out.

The energy vibrations and the light from within the crystal—the energy vibrations within you, within your mind—are becoming stronger and more clearly defined, completely opening up inside you and expanding into multidimensional realms of insight, knowing, and awareness.

There are some very special fringe benefits to this meditation that you may have just discovered, and will definitely discover the more you work with it to strengthen your innate powers of inner seeing and sensing (insight and intuition.)

In addition to helping you learn how to visualize—to see with your mind's eye—and to intuitively sense, through your inner perceptions, by illuminating the imagery of your thoughts and feelings, this meditation also shows you how you energize and express your thoughts and feelings in and through all your experiences—how they first become real in your mind and then manifest in your life, showing you how you create your reality.

This meditation also helps you to clearly see and understand the symbols and imagery in both your dreams and your everyday experiences, and to accurately interpret them.

As is true with all the meditations in this book, you'll discover more than what is apparent on the surface and just below it—you'll travel deeper and further than that. There's much more to experience and know. Explore and enjoy.

# Hidden Horizons

—————————— ℘ ——————————

*As you walk along the beach, you
gaze out to the horizon, wondering
what is beyond your line of vision.*

Walking along the beach, you look at the horizon where the water
meets the sky, wondering what is beyond your line of vision. You
think you'd like to go exploring to discover what's really out there—
what's beyond your conscious knowing—but you think it's impossi-
ble to swim that far.

But what if you could? What if there was a way? It's just a
thought, but you entertain the idea, curious to know. You put your
toes in the water; it's warm and welcoming.

As you continue walking along the beach by the edge of the
shore, splashing your feet in the water, you happen upon a small but
sturdy boat. This offers you some wonderful choices and an exciting
opportunity.

You can decide to stay by the shore and wonder what the horizon
holds. You're having a very pleasant experience here and you may
want to just enjoy it more completely, to think about what might be
beyond the horizon and to ponder the possibilities.

You can decide to go for a short sail, drifting through the waves
close to shore, seeing things you're familiar and comfortable with,
becoming more aware of them, and enjoying the rhythm and motion
of the water and the waves.

You can decide to be swept out to sea, gently flowing and floating in this safe, secure boat that can take you into uncharted waters, perhaps into other realms and realities of perception and awareness that will allow you to see and explore a bigger, broader perspective, where you can expand your consciousness to experience things you may have never seen before or perhaps have just never noticed, or to experience them in a different way.

You can experience this meditation in several ways. You can use it as a visualization to gain more information to help you understand the challenges and choices you're facing in your physical reality, to give yourself some distance from them so you can clearly tune into your true thoughts and feelings, and to get a better look at the overall picture of your experiences.

If you're ready to take risks or are thinking about making some changes in your life, you can sail away to sea [see] their possible and probable outcomes before they're played out in your reality, and to change things that have not yet occurred. When you return to shore [sure], you may discover that things are very different than they first appeared to be.

If you feel adventuresome, you can use this visualization to encourage and self-empower you on your path of self-discovery and spiritual awareness. You decide where you want to go and how far you want to travel into and perhaps beyond the hidden horizons of your mind.

Or you can simply set sail and see what happens. This meditation works for a little leap of faith as well as a giant lunge of trust. You can go beyond the boundaries of your conscious reality, beyond the physical structure of time and space into the infinite multidimensionality of your soul.

# Canvas of Creation

———————— ∾ ————————

*You're in an artist's studio where there are many colors
of paints, brushes, and blank canvasses for you to create
all the experiences you'd like to have in your life.*

Looking around the artist's studio, you see hundreds of canvasses and tubes of paint. Ideas begin to sparkle inside your imagination as you think about what you'd like to create and experience. You know this is a special studio and that you can come here whenever you want to paint more pictures into your life.

Perhaps your studio is open and airy. Perhaps it has a skylight and sliding glass doors around every side that open into a beautiful nature scene, maybe a garden or a meadow or a magical forest. Perhaps it's a large, spacious loft with lots of room for all the many pictures—the masterpieces—that you know you'll create here.

Maybe your artist's studio is a frame of mind, a magical place of insight, inspiration, thought, and wonder in your creative awareness. Or perhaps it's somewhere in the universe, a special place that is illuminated with a mystical light.

Looking inside your imagination—inside your thoughts and feelings—you feel magically inspired as you begin to paint some of the pictures you'd like to experience in your life, filling in details with descriptive images and flashes of insight.

Delighted, you discover you have a real flair and talent for this. As you allow the artist in you to emerge and come forth, you feel a wonderful power building within you as you realize you can create whatever you want, and that you hold within your mind and your hands all the creative tools you need to sketch and draw, and shape and sculpt the many images and expressions of your experiences.

Pausing for a moment, you stand back to admire your work. Looking at your partially-completed pictures to study what you've just created and to decide how to enhance them and what finishing touches and flourishes you'd like to add, you notice that somehow, magically, the canvasses have begun to come to life and to become the experiences you painted.

They're three-dimensional as they move and begin to become your experiences. They're living, breathing, being and becoming images and expressions of your thoughts and the feelings that created them. You see both the illusionary and the tangible nature of your thoughts, and how they become real first in your mind and then in the manifest world.

The pictures—the tones and hues of the colors—are ever-changing in every moment, influenced by your choices, and by every nuance of your thoughts and feelings.

Every action and reaction you have changes and thereby affects and alters your original ideas, insights, and experiences, creating new and various expressions to the work of art that is your life in motion.

# Babbling Brook

*This stream of water has many magical things to
say to you and many wonderful things to show you.*

You're walking beside a flowing stream of water, a gently-rippling brook which makes gentle, harmonious sounds that are music to your ears. The clear, pure sparkling water is filled with lovely, healing, nurturing sounds. Somehow you know this stream of water, this stream of subconsciousness, flows in harmony with your spirit, and that the water has many magical things to say to you and many wonderful things to show you and share with you.

Continuing to walk beside the babbling brook, noticing the sparkles and shimmers of sunlight on the water that are reflected in your soul, you find a peaceful place to sit and meditate.

Listen to the gentle, harmonious sounds all around you—to the flow of the water over the pebbles and small ledges in the brook, hearing the song it sings to you as it creates a blissful, beautiful harmony in your mind.

You can hear the brook as it talks to you and shares the secrets of life with you. It sings to you about the harmony and interrelationship of the many worlds within the energies of itself and the earth, about the realms of knowing within your mind.

Deciding to continue your walk, you follow the stream of water—the stream of life—as it journeys on its way, as you journey on your path through the experiences in your life, listening to the gentle, harmonious sound of the water as it rushes and bubbles and splashes along its path, communicating with you and sharing the knowledge of its journey as it listens to you sharing your journey.

You realize this brook is simply going with the flow, just as you are. Sometimes meandering on its path, sometimes flowing and rushing forth, sometimes at a standstill, setting a new course of direction, sometimes detouring around rocks and boulders, sometimes building enough power to overflow a temporary blockage, it continues its natural flow.

At times, it's a clear, sparkling stream, at other times, it's a still, quiet pool of water reflecting the sky and the universe, reflecting your thoughts and feelings as you look into the water. With a gentle breeze as soft as a whisper, it ripples into infinity, into eternity, into the knowledge inside your soul.

# Cushiony Clouds

———————— ❧ ————————

*Be inside a puffy white cloud in the
sky; sink into its cushiony softness as
you float leisurely along, free and light.*

You're outside on a beautiful, warm, sunny day, lying in a softly-swaying hammock, enjoying the gentle breeze and the warmth and light of the sunshine. Looking up at the sky, you see a few puffy white clouds floating leisurely by, and you notice how blue and expansive the sky is.

You wonder what it would be like to float through the sky on a puffy white cloud. Would it be the same as swinging in your hammock or would it be completely different? Would it change your perceptions or perspective of things? Would it help clear some cloudiness in your mind, and open a higher understanding?

Using your imagination, you project yourself into the sky, onto that puffy white cloud. Feeling free and light, weightless, unrestrained by gravity, you're floating along, carefree and happy. The cloud supports you with a cushiony softness that is unlike anything you've ever experienced.

As the cloud floats along, directed by unseen universal winds, you begin to wonder where it's going, but this thought doesn't really concern you. You're quite content to just go with the flow, to be completely here now in the present moment, to experience the calm, relaxing feeling of simply floating on the gentle breeze.

Every once in a while, you peer over the side of the cloud and look down at the earth, knowing you can return at any time and that you're perfectly safe where you are.

Even though the cloud seems to be drifting in the wind, you know there's a universal direction it follows, a natural flow of energy, and that this cloud has its own purpose for being.

You wonder what that purpose might be, so you merge your consciousness with the cloud's consciousness to discover its reason for existence. Inside its misty, ethereal appearance as a wispy white cloud, it has a definite purpose for being. It's always there, in one form or another, fulfilling its divine purpose.

Seemingly floating aimlessly along, it has seen and experienced many wonderful and magical things. It has traveled the world in many forms: Sometimes as the puffy white cloud it is now floating softly on a gentle breeze. Sometimes seeming to disappear and dissipate in the light of the sun, changing its shape and substance, reappearing when it draws moisture from the earth, being nourished from its physical source, and in turn, nurturing the earth with universal energy.

Sometimes it appears as a powerful dark cloud, rolling and roaring through the sky as it thunders and creates bold streaks of lightning, invigorating and energizing the earth. Sometimes pouring rain, at other times offering a gentle shower of rain, sharing universal nourishment with the earth.

You become aware that even though at times it may seem that your life appears to be like this puffy white cloud as it is expressing itself at this moment, seemingly drifting aimlessly along, there is a unique and very special purpose you have in life and perhaps you're just floating along for the moment, either relaxing or gathering information and energy that will manifest in another form for a particular purpose.

Perfectly content to travel gently on this puffy white cloud in the sky, you continue to float along, thinking your thoughts and knowing that everything you do and experience is part of a perfect plan you've created for yourself, that all the events in your life have a very special purpose and meaning, and a reason for existence.

There are many other things this cloud can tell you and share with you, and many special, magical things it can show and offer you. This cloud is your magic carpet ride to anywhere you want to go and is also a mentor for your thoughts.

Just like the cloud, you're going with the flow, sometimes merging with other clouds, sometimes floating free and alone, just enjoying the journey of being here now, in the present moment. You think about how wonderful and free this cloud is, about how wonderful and free you are.

Suddenly, you're back in your hammock, swaying softly in the gentle breeze, looking up at the puffy white clouds in the sky, knowing the mysteries of your mind and how powerful and truly awesome your awareness is.

You smile to yourself, knowing you've discovered something very wonderful and magical. You've learned how to see through your physical reality from a higher, spiritual perspective. You've discovered that your consciousness exists separately from your physical body, and your thoughts are free to travel on the energy of air inside what appears to be a cushiony white mist of illusion in the sky.

# Special Swan

&

*Fly into the magical realms of your dreams and*
*discover how to make all your dreams come true.*

You feel as if you're dreaming. You're somewhere inside a dream, in a dream within a dream, dreaming about a beautiful white swan who has the magical ability to carry you into the realms of your dreams and to fly you anywhere you desire to visit.

Inside this misty image of a dream, you see yourself in a peaceful place in nature, next to a beautiful lake. Looking out over the water, you notice how it ripples gently in the soft breeze.

Closing your eyes, you let yourself fully experience the gentle, warm breeze as it softly caresses you. You hear the ripples on the water and think perhaps it is because of the breeze, but something inside you whispers it is more than the gentle wind, more than a dream.

Opening your eyes, you see the beautiful white swan you were dreaming about has just landed gracefully on the water, which caused the ripples you heard. She swims over to you, welcoming you as if you are a dear friend she hasn't seen for a long time.

Magically, because you know you're dreaming, you know you can communicate with her. You begin to converse with her, telling her of your dreams, your hopes, your desires. You know, in a special place inside your dreams, that you've done this many times before and that she is your dream mentor.

She tells you she is here to help you, that she can transport you into the land of your dreams. She swims very close to you so you may climb on her back to fly away into the magical world of dreams. At first, you think your weight will be too much for her, but she assures you she is magical and can transport your spirit with ease. She reminds you that your dreaming self is as free and light as the wind.

As you climb on her back, she takes wing and flies into the clouds, then above the clouds into a universal realm of dreams. As she flies, your spirit takes wing and begins to soar alongside your swan, sharing your journey together. She guides you to a special place where the dreams you dream inside your soul are real and shows you how to make them real in your life.

Spend some time in this magical place to see how you can make your dreams come true. When you are ready to leave, your swan guides your spirit back to your earth reality.

She bids you good-bye at the water's edge and says she will return to you, whenever you wish to travel into the land of your dreams. You smile at her, thanking her for the journey she has taken you on, and the path she has shown you inside your dreams.

As you awaken, you know this is more than just a dream.

# Secluded Serenity

─────────── ൭ ───────────

*Be in a secluded cove by a quiet, calm pool*
*of water. Feel the tranquility nurture your*
*mind and your body as it nourishes your soul.*

Create an image of a peaceful, calm pool of water in a secluded cove. See the lush greenery and flowering bushes that surround you. Perhaps there's a gently-swaying palm tree that moves gracefully in the gentle breeze as its branches touch the water.

This is a perfectly peaceful place in nature, a quiet, soothing, relaxing, safe place where you can be alone—a sanctuary all your own. It's beautiful and untouched; no one has ever been here before. You're the first and only person to have set foot here.

It's a sacred space you can experience and enjoy. It's a special, serene place where you can refresh your mind and replenish the spiritual energies of your soul.

There's a magical essence in this place of secluded serenity, a mystical feel and sense to this beautiful place in nature. It has an aura about it, an ambiance and charm that you resonate perfectly to with every part of you.

Feel the tranquility of this secluded place in nature nurture your mind and body, and nourish your soul. Let your mind be still, free from all the cares and worries of the outside world.

# Reflections

༄

*Follow a sparkling stream of water in the center of
a lush, beautiful valley to see where the path leads you.*

You're standing at the rim of a gently-sloping valley. Looking into
the valley, you see the sun radiating sparkles of light from a softly-
winding stream of water in the center. The gentle breeze and warmth
of the day invite you for a walk.

Noticing a footpath leading down through the lush, flowering
bushes into the verdant valley below, you decide to follow the path
to see where it leads. As you walk, admiring the beauty and appreciating the tranquility all around you, you sense this same feeling of
peace within you, and you know you've found the path that leads you
within to your spiritual self.

You're in the center of the valley by the sparkling stream of water. Standing here for a few moments to simply enjoy being in this
beautiful, peaceful place in nature, you listen to the gentle sounds of
nature all around you—to the flow of the water over the small pebbles
in the brook, hearing the song it sings to you and the unspoken words
in your soul, hearing and feeling the soft sound of the wind as it whispers quietly through the leaves of the trees beside you, creating a
blissful, beautiful harmony, as the sounds of nature speak softly to
your heart, mind, and soul.

You feel so completely natural and comfortable here, tranquil
and at home, totally in tune with nature and centered within yourself.

Closing your eyes for a moment, you deeply breathe in the pure, clean air, completely experiencing and sensing nature all around you, bringing it deeply within yourself—being fully in and reconnecting with nature, with every part of you—feeling the joy, peace, and harmony. Opening your eyes, you smile at the wonder-filled world around you and within you.

Taking your shoes off, you feel the soft, luxuriant grass beneath your bare feet, as the earth shares its soft, nurturing essence with you. You feel the gentle, caressing energy of the earth vibrating quietly and softly.

You hear the music of the water as it flows in a gentle stream. Noticing the water is ankle deep, you step into it, feeling it softly move around your feet and through your toes. The water is cool and refreshing; it feels wonderful on your skin as it gently surges and swirls around your feet.

Standing in this sparkling, gently-swirling stream of water, you feel rejuvenated and sense the energy of your spiritual nature rising up within you, becoming open and expansive and free. Laughing with happiness, you kneel down closer to the water, listening to it gently ripple and flow over and around the pebbles you can clearly see beneath the surface.

Joyfully splashing the water all around you with your hands, you feel that same surge of gentle energy vibrate through your hands, and you notice how the drops of water catch the sunlight and radiate rainbows.

Slowly and thoughtfully, you stand up and walk through the water to a quiet pool you see a few steps away. You look up into the azure-blue sky, seeing the soft wisps of a few billowy white clouds floating leisurely above you, and you feel the warmth of the sun gently caressing your face and skin.

Looking down at the still, calm pool of water, you notice how the sunshine sparkles and shimmers on the water, reflecting the blueness of the sky and the white wispiness of the clouds. Looking into the clear, sparkling water, you see the pebbles beneath the surface. A gentle breeze ripples the water, softly caressing it.

Stepping out of the water and kneeling down to look into the pool, you see more than the reflection of your physical self on the mirror-like surface of the water. Shimmering in the water is the essence of your inner, spiritual self, moving around and through your image in gentle ripples. You notice how the water reflects and mirrors the sunlight and the sky above you, and you recognize that your physical self is really a mirror of your spiritual self.

At the same time, you realize that the reality of your everyday experiences go much deeper than your conscious mind, much farther than the physical world. Below the surface of every thought and feeling, and all around you in every experience, your spiritual self waits, ever so quietly, to be recognized, to be heard.

Sitting beside the sparkling stream of water in this beautiful verdant valley, you begin to listen quietly to your thoughts, to your inner voice, just as you earlier listened to the quiet sounds of nature, feeling and hearing them all around you and within you at the same time. You feel completely at home here, centered in your heart and mind, and connected with your essence, in tune with your true nature.

You know that the voice you hear in your mind is your spiritual self whispering softly to you in your thoughts and feelings, and through your dreams and experiences. As you listen, you know you can feel and be completely aware of all the many expressions and ripples of your experiences as you travel through them, joyfully following the path that leads you within.

# Key to Knowledge

*In a huge hallway, you see a door, illuminated with an aura of light, that is waiting for you to open it. Somewhere inside your mind, you find a magical key that unlocks all the doors to your awareness, showing you the magic and power of your mind.*

You're somewhere in the universe in a huge hallway with arched ceilings. A radiant light emanates from everywhere around you, illuminating the doorways that line the hall, extending farther than the eye can see. Wondering what is inside each room, you try to open the first door on your right but discover to your dismay that it's locked.

Undaunted and more curious now to know what is inside, you pause to think as you contemplate this dilemma for a moment. Considering where you are and why you're here, and what you've been looking for in your life, you intuitively know the doors open into all the magical, wonderful worlds within yourself, into the magic and power of your mind, into your inner knowing and your spiritual awareness, and that within each room are the secrets to your soul and the answers to all the mysteries of the universe.

Determined to find a way inside and wishing you had a key, you feel a warm tingle in your hand—a vibration of energy—and you hear a popping sound. In a flashing sparkle of light, an ornate golden key appears in your hand. This seems so miraculous to you—that the key magically appeared out of nowhere the moment you wished for it.

Turning it over in your hand, feeling its warmth and energy, then cupping it in the palm of your hand, caressing it with the fingers of your other hand, you know this is a most wondrous and powerful key because it opens the doors to all the magic and knowledge inside your mind and offers you the treasures of truth. At the same time, you know you've always held within you the key that could open up your mind and your spiritual awareness.

You insert the key into the lock and stand there for a moment, enjoying the wonderful feeling of happy anticipation and joy within you, knowing you're about to begin a very wonderful inner journey. Turning the key, the door opens easily.

Crossing the threshold, you enter the room with a feeling of respect and awe, knowing you have gained access to universal wisdom and knowledge, and that you're now able to discover and explore all the wonders of the many worlds within you, to discover everything you've always wanted to know and more.

You know you've given yourself a special, magical, wonderful gift—that you hold the key to knowledge in your hand—a key that gives you entry into your inner, spiritual self and opens the doors into all your knowledge, into the multidimensional worlds of the universe both within you and all around you.

# Little Lost Leaf

—————————— ✆ ——————————

*Walking on a beautiful autumn day, you
notice a vibrant, colorful leaf that has lost its
connection to the tree and fallen to the ground.*

It's a beautiful autumn day, clear and crisp and sunny. You're outside
for a walk, going nowhere in particular, just walking for exercise and
enjoyment, and to get your thoughts clear on changes you're thinking
about making in your life. Perhaps you feel a bit lost or disconnected,
as if you've outgrown something and you're searching for a new
sense of direction, a new way to grow.

You look at the changing leaves on the trees that are very colorful
and vibrant. You notice that a little leaf has fallen to the ground. It
calls to you, asking to be noticed, wanting to share its essence with
you. It's very beautiful and unusual, a very unique and individual,
multicolored leaf—orange and red and yellow.

Picking it up, perhaps feeling a bit sad at first that it has lost its
connection to the tree, you soon begin to realize it is following its
course of direction and purpose, beginning a new journey that ulti-
mately leads to renewal and growth.

You compare this leaf to yourself and to the changing seasons, to
the changes in life. Perhaps you are going through changes in your
life, maybe feeling a little sad and lost yourself as you make changes,
let go of connections, and prepare for new directions and new journeys in your life. Perhaps you've outgrown something and it is time

to move on, to explore new options and choices. Perhaps you're unsure of your direction.

You look at the leaf and notice it is ready to move forward in its life cycle—saying good-bye, letting go with love. You admire its courage, knowing you must find that same courage within yourself to move on. You relate to this leaf and feel a deep, inner sense of kinship and familiarity with it. Like you, the leaf has outgrown this particular connection.

You look at the tree it has fallen from and feel a sincere gratefulness and appreciation for the growth this leaf has experienced, for the growth you've experienced, for the connection that enabled you to grow and flourish, and now to move on to a new direction in your life—a new course of exploration and growth.

You begin to explore your inner essence, going within yourself to see the changes you're contemplating in your life, to renew and revitalize yourself, making ready to burst forth anew, allowing the budding and blossoming of your soul to renew itself from deep within.

# Special Spring Morning

*Enjoy a beautiful Spring morning as the world wakes
up and renews itself. Feel your own reawakening as you
see your spiritual growth opening up and blossoming.*

It's a wonder-filled, beautiful day, an incredibly special Spring morning when the world is waking up from its winter's sleep.

Breathing in the pure, clean freshness of the air, you smell the wonderful scents of the earth renewing itself, bursting forth and blossoming with life. You notice the greenness all around you and the tender buds and blossoms on the trees and bushes as they begin to embrace their reawakening, opening up and welcoming their new beginnings.

You notice how the earth is waking up all around you, creating sparkling colors and splashes of splendor everywhere you look. You're totally enjoying the feeling of being alive on such a wonderfully beautiful day with its promise of renewal and growth, its vibrancy and essence.

Everything is beautiful and bursting with life. It's an extraordinary day, filled with joy and sunshine and gentle warmth. Looking around and taking it all in, you feel so very happy to be part of this glorious day, to see and experience the beauty of it everywhere you look. You feel completely at one with nature, with the world around you, and you sense the world within you waking up.

The bushes and trees are covered with buds and blossoms moving in the gentle breeze; they're beginning to grow their leaves, renewing themselves from deep within, birthing and bringing forth new life. You notice the interplay and dance of sunlight on and in and through the new greenness of the trees and bushes and flowers, how the light gently touches and caresses each bud, each blossom, each new leaf, welcoming it forth.

Feeling the gentle warmth of the sun on your face and skin, and the breeze as it caresses you softly, you listen to the harmonious sounds you hear—the sound of birds chirping as if they are welcoming the new growth, and the breeze singing through the leaves on the trees. You hear the sunshine sparkling all around you.

You're hearing the sounds of nature coming alive, bursting forth, blossoming and blooming with buds and vibrantly green growth that offers you the promise of new beginnings as you listen to the eternal essence of life.

Looking at the sparkling dewdrops on the lush, green grass and on the tips of the leaves on the bushes, you notice delicate rainbows sparkling with life, radiating multicolored auras that touch the leaves and blades of grass softly, caressingly, playing in the sunshine. It's almost as if the rainbows are alive, expressing their joy at the beauty and renewal of life, and feeling blessed to be part of this beautiful day.

Looking at the early flowers in bloom, at their intricacy and detail, and the delicate profusion and variety of buds on the trees and bushes, you touch them gently and lovingly, feeling their texture and smelling their wonderful fragrance and aroma. You see every detail of them, noticing the hues and tones of color, each nuance and form.

You see how they're beginning to open up, and you feel that same sense of your essence opening up within you, showing you all the beauty you have inside you and expressing the joy of your soul on this beautiful, magical Spring morning.

You know your spirit is coming alive again, and you know you're part of all the things you feel and see, and sense and hear and know, and experience as you enjoy all the scents and sounds of this wonder-filled Spring morning with every part of you.

But most of all, you are completely aware of your spiritual renewal and rejuvenation on this beautiful day of new beginnings. You feel your inner essence, your spirituality, reawakening into the vibrant, radiant light and joy of life—beginning to blossom and grow—renewing your aliveness from deep within and opening up your soul to new levels of awareness.

You feel your spirit reawakening as it is nourished and nurtured from the light of the sun and from the light within you. Breathing in the light, you feel your own spiritual renewal, your transformation and growth, your inner essence opening up and springing forth, blossoming and growing, bursting forth in your life.

# Vision Quest

_____ ✑ _____

*Take a nature trek through a tropical rain forest
where you search for and find what you are seeking.*

You begin to follow a path that leads you into a tropical rain forest
that is lush and green, overflowing with the essence of life. Beams
and shafts of light filter through the thick canopy of leaves that open
to the sky in bright blue splashes and glimpses of pure white clouds.
You feel a subdued sense of quiet in this sacred place; you also feel
a sense of adventure within you as you walk forward on your vision
quest.

Perhaps you clearly know what you are seeking or you know
you'll recognize it when you see it, or perhaps your vision quest is
open to whatever you experience on this journey of your soul for
knowledge. Trusting that you will find what you are searching for,
you continue to go deeper within.

Clouds begin to gather; you hear the distant rumble of thunder
and see occasional bright flashes of lightning. You can smell the scent
of rain in the air. It is becoming darker as the rain approaches, but
you feel safe guided by your soul, knowing you are on a spiritual
vision quest. You feel intimately connected with this forest, this place
of sacredness you have entered.

As the rain begins to drop softly, you hear the gentle patter on the
leaves. You see the water dripping from the tips of the leaves and

smell the rich scent of the wet earth as you feel the moisture in the air all around you.

You close your eyes for a moment to completely experience and absorb the feel of the rain on your skin and the warm, gentle breeze, listening to the sound of the raindrops on the leaves. You become one with the essence of the rain, the scent of the earth, the feel of the air, and with the leaves as they are touched and nourished by the rain.

As suddenly as it began, the rain stops and the sun bursts forth, sparkling with light and radiating dazzling rainbows on the water dripping from the leaves. Even with your eyes closed, you see the vibrancy and feel the energy and aura of the tropical rain forest.

Opening your eyes and looking all around, you know you're experiencing the essence of life, the sharing of the universe with the earth, seeing how the universe nourishes the earth, how it nurtures the life that is growing there. You become aware of how your soul— your spirit—shares with you and nourishes you.

Continuing on your vision quest, walking the path through the rain forest—the path that leads you within to your soul, to your essence—you come to a tall tree with a door in its trunk, an open door that beckons you within.

Knowing you're completely safe, you enter. Although you expected it to be dark, you see that it is lit with a radiant light from within that glows everywhere, illuminating everything it touches. This light has a special feeling and quality to it, an ambiance and essence that is both tangible and intangible at the same time. The light opens up feelings inside you that are at once familiar and foreign to you. Then you begin to remember, to know all that is within you.

You see a magical, mystical world opening up and unfolding before you. Gazing joyfully all around you, you know you've found what your soul was searching for and that your vision quest has shown you the way to a special place inside your soul, a sacred space that offers you many treasures and gifts of insight and wisdom, a spiritual place that is your sanctuary, and within this sanctuary you become aware of many things your soul has always known.

Perhaps there is a guide who has been waiting for you who now comes forward to greet you, to walk with you through this wonder-filled world, to show and share with you many experiences your soul desires to have. Perhaps you recognize this guide as a spiritual friend you've traveled with before or perhaps this guide is a new friend who has a special connection with you.

Or perhaps you have a knowingness that this guide is your higher self, who has been waiting, ever so patiently and lovingly, for you to become aware of the true essence of yourself—your soul—and to re-member all the spiritual knowledge you have within you.

Explore and experience every part of this sacred place within yourself. Allow your guide to take you wherever you want to go, to be both your companion and your way-shower as you find everything you're looking for on your vision quest that leads you into your soul.

# Being at the Beach

※

*Tune into the rhythm of the tide and the
motion of harmony, as you experience perfect
contentment and peace all around you and within you.*

It's a warm, sunny day and you're at the beach. Listening to the splash of the waves and the sound of the water as it comes to the shore, you hear the gentle motion of the waves and you're aware of the eternal essence of the tides as they ebb and flow.

As you walk along the beach, you feel the softness and warmth of the sand beneath your feet. Perhaps you notice a few seashells that have been washed ashore by the tide and you pick them up to admire them.

As you continue walking along the beach, you see a perfect place to relax next to some large rocks that stretch across the sand. As you get comfortable on your towel, you feel the sand adjust to your body. As you lie on the beach, you feel the warmth of the sun on your skin as it gently permeates your body.

The sky is an azure-blue, with a few puffy white clouds floating leisurely by. The sun is bright and strong, and feels pleasantly warm on your body. You feel a gentle breeze and smell the scent of the salt spray from the ocean.

You hear the sound of seagulls and the muted talk and laughter of other people in the distance. You feel so relaxed and peaceful; the quiet hum of conversation sounds like soft, gentle music.

As you lie on the beach, you listen to the water as it comes to the shore and as it returns to the ocean. As the tide ebbs and flows, your breathing begins to match the rhythm of the tide—in and out, back and forth.

You feel yourself relaxing completely. You feel perfectly content and peaceful as you listen to the gentle sound of the waves. You're just relaxing, tuning into your inner self, flowing into your spirit.

The sound of the ocean is lulling, soothing, and relaxing. The sounds ebb and flow, forming a gentle, rhythmic pattern that moves in tune with your thoughts and feelings. The sun is pleasantly warm on your body and the sound of the ocean completely relaxes you. All your thoughts flow into a gentle awareness of this beautiful day.

You feel a wonderful contentment and peace. You're enjoying the warmth of the sun and the rhythm of the tide; you're in harmony with everything you're experiencing.

# Part Two

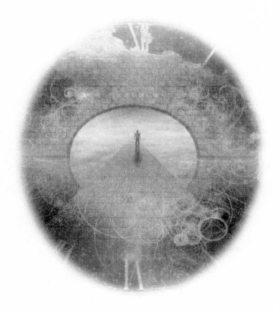

*Magical Meditations*

**Part Two** centers on the theme of the interrelationship and harmony with the earth and the universe. Inside this part, you'll find magical meditations and visualizations to make your heart happy, to make your mind more open and aware, and to make your soul sing.

These meditations share with you a way to rediscover and reawaken all the magic you have within you. They invite you to reach within, to embrace your inner self—to stretch above and beyond yourself into your soul—to remember the knowledge of the universe, the secrets of nature and the earth, and to share your essence and harmony with the earth and the universe as you reconnect with yourself.

These meditations offer you a way to bring the physical and spiritual worlds together and blend them into your everyday world, into every experience in your life. They hold the promise of reunions with the spiritual side of yourself, if you will look within your heart, mind, and soul to remember, rediscover, and recognize the magic that already exists within you.

# Magical Melodies

＿＿＿＿＿＿＿＿  ❧  ＿＿＿＿＿＿＿＿

*Listen to the music inside your mind as it lightly
vibrates into your thoughts and feelings, plays gently
through your heart, and softly sings into your soul.*

You enter a quiet, warmly-lit room that appears to be empty, yet you sense—you know—there is a wonderful treasure here, a very special, spiritual gift that drew you to this subdued, magical room.

Looking around, you notice a small, delicately-decorated music box, set with amethyst crystals that radiate the colors of a rainbow. Opening it, you hear a beautiful melody begin to play.

You listen to the peaceful, gentle, soothing melody of harmony that softly flows inside your soul. The sounds are harmonious and gentle, soft and soothing, bringing you into a peaceful place within yourself. It's the most beautiful music you've ever heard.

Delighted, you close your eyes to more fully experience and appreciate the music as it richly fills every part of the acoustically-perfect room—as it fills all your senses and every part of your awareness with pure enjoyment as it reverberates softly into and through your body, mind, heart, and soul.

The music fills you with harmonious tones of a beautiful melody, softly flowing into, around, and through your soul. The song is caressing and comforting, healing and soothing. The melody of the music brings forth a wonderful feeling of joy inside you as you feel and hear the rhythm that is in harmony with your soul as the melody vibrates through you and within you.

The melody is somehow familiar to you. You know that the tones and chords you're hearing are the sacred song of your soul, flowing and resonating deep within you and all around you. The music is filled with the harmony of the vibrations of your soul, bringing you into a beautiful place of inner peace, a place of joy and light.

You listen with every part of you, to the peaceful, gentle, soothing melody of harmony that softly flows into and through you, as it lightly resonates into your thoughts and feelings, plays gently through your heart, and softly sings into your soul, then you close your eyes to fully absorb the sound within.

The music flows in you and through you, filling every part of you with harmony, resonating with every part of your awareness. You're in a sacred space of peace and harmony where you're in perfect rhythm and tune with your spiritual essence.

As you completely tune into the harmony of the tones, and the sounds of the feelings that the music inspires and brings forth within you, you feel yourself—your awareness—expanding ever so softly and gently into the rhythm and tune and melody of your spiritual essence.

As your awareness expands into the music, it becomes part of you. It's as if you are the music; you are the melody. You know that the music you hear comes from a place of memory deep within you, from the knowingness of your soul. The music plays the celestial song of the universe—the symphony of your soul.

Your soul has listened to the music many times before; the music is a gentle reminder of your true spiritual nature. The notes in this universal song share with you all the mysteries in your mind; the melody reveals the secrets of your soul.

As you listen to the music in your mind, you hear it with your heart as it flows inside your soul. The song sings to you of home, calling to you softly and gently. This magical, mystical music box plays a melody of harmony, peace, and love within you—the natural vibration of your soul.

The song of your soul caresses and envelopes you every day with its magical melody and sound, touching every part of your life. You can hear the pure joy of your soul singing to you in shimmers and waves of light.

You know that the sacred song of your soul is in every part of you, in every part of your life, and that when you listen, you can hear the harmony of your soul everywhere around you, in every moment, in every experience.

Your soul sings to you in the morning, in the colors of a beautiful sunrise of a new day. You hear it flowing through the leaves of the trees, whispering to you. You feel the melody in the soft, gentle touch of the wind on your face, and the warm caress of sunlight. You see the harmony of your sacred song in every beautiful flower when you breathe in its wonderful scent.

The music now begins to softly ebb, lingering like beautiful, melodious wind chimes dancing in a gentle breeze, echoing within your soul. Even though the music is now silent, you know you can listen to the song of your soul any time you want to, simply by listening in silence.

# Garden of Harmony

―――――― ✿ ――――――

*Be in a beautiful garden filled with lush, green plants
and flowers that vibrate with health and harmony.*

Being in a beautiful garden is beneficial for your health. It promotes peace and harmony, both inside your mind and in your body, as well as uplifting your spirit.

As you read through, and then do, this meditation in your mind or outside in nature, open your imagination; enhance the meditation and add to it all the special things in nature you resonate with—the feelings that inspire and bring peace and harmony to you, and the images you feel connected to in a happy, healing way. Change the meditation in any way you want to, so it truly reflects what a garden of harmony is to you.

You may want to read this meditation when you're outside in a special place in nature where you truly feel connected with nature, so you can completely feel the healing energies of nature with every part of you—within your body, mind, and spirit—and where you can experience the vibrations of health and harmony with all your physical and spiritual senses.

―――――― ✿ ――――――

You're in a very beautiful garden. Looking around, you see lush, flowering bushes filled with flowers and blooms—delicate orchids and multicolored wildflowers, spread among open, spacious, grassy areas. The fragrance of the flowers is lovely and pleasing; the purity of their colors is awe-inspiring.

You look at the bright, colorful, vibrant flowers swaying softly in the gentle breeze. Their colors are magnificent—shimmering and iridescent at the same time. The bushes and flowers move gently in the soft, warm breeze, creating balance and beauty within the garden and within your mind. The garden emanates a vibrant feeling of energy, radiant and abundant with life and health.

Everything in your garden vibrates in harmony, in tune with nature. It's quiet and peaceful, and the air is clean and pure and refreshing.

Deeply breathing in the peace and harmony of this beautiful, spiritual garden, you sense the oneness of the garden with nature, and you sense that same oneness within yourself as you begin to absorb the harmony and the healing energies of the garden within your body, your mind, and your spirit.

The day is filled with warm sunshine and a brilliant blue sky above you. The light and warmth of the sun on your face and body feels wonderful and rejuvenating. The grass beneath your bare feet feels soft and luxuriant.

The healing colors of the blue sky and the green grass surround you, enveloping you with a calm, gentle, soothing, peaceful feeling. The warmth from the sun's rays begin to permeate and radiate through you, filling you with a wonderful feeling of health and harmony. You feel perfectly in tune with nature and with the universal energies of sunlight.

Within your garden, you feel drawn to a very special place of peace and harmony where you feel most in tune with the healing energies of sunlight and nature all around you. As you enter this special healing place in your garden, you feel completely at peace with yourself and totally in harmony with the beauty and serenity all around you.

In this special healing place in your garden, you feel the vibrations of energy that are both around you and within you. As you center in on the warmth and light from the sun, you feel the healing energies of sunlight gently vibrating all around you, flowing through you and within you.

Breathe in the sunlight; breathe in the greenness of the earth and the blueness of the sky. Breathe the health and harmony of this beautiful garden deeply inside you—into every part of your body, your mind, and your spirit.

Feel your mind, your thoughts and feelings, and your body vibrating in harmony with the light, totally in tune with both your physical and your spiritual nature, completely in tune with the peaceful, healing energies of your garden. Experience and enjoy the perfect health and harmony you feel within yourself—within your body, your mind, and your spirit.

While this meditation is very gentle, the healing energies are very powerful. Bring the peace and harmony you feel within every part of you, and the radiant vibrations of light and health you've just experienced, into your conscious mind and let them softly flow through your thoughts and feelings, and your body, over and over again.

Allow this Garden of Harmony to become a special place of healing for you whenever you need it, or when you just want to be in a pleasant place to enjoy serenity and peace of mind.

# A Magical Place

―――――――――― ⸙ ――――――――――

*Go inside the wonderful world of your
imagination and find your inner child
that you left behind a long time ago.*

Remember a treasured, private place you enjoyed and explored as a
child—a special, secret space that no one else knew about—a place
you could go when you wanted to be with yourself, perhaps to be
alone with your thoughts and feelings.

Your magical place is where you enjoyed being peaceful, safe,
and happy within yourself, where you could truly be who you really
are. A place where you could tune into yourself, and to connect with
the inner, vital part of you—your inner child who is now all grown
up into your inner self.

This magical place in your mind is where you can reconnect with
yourself, where you can reunite with the carefree, innocent, loving,
joyous parts of yourself to experience the child-like wonder that you
knew before. It's a place where you can nourish your soul and experience total harmony within yourself. It's the place that waits for you
to remember it and visit it again.

Perhaps, when you were a child, it was a real place or perhaps it
only seemed to exist somewhere inside your imagination. Smiling,
you begin to remember this special place in your childhood memory,
and you also remember your very special imaginary friend who was

always there for you, waiting for you to come to your special, magical place to play in your imagination.

You think about the imaginary friend you had as a child, your special playmate who lived in a very private place inside your imagination. Even though no one else believed he/she was real, you knew, in a magical place in your heart and deep inside your soul, that your friend was just as real as you are.

Somehow, though, you lost touch with your special friend, but you never truly forgot him/her or all the good times you both shared. You think about the times he/she cheered you up when you felt sad and the way your friend would magically appear out of nowhere when you most needed him/her, or if you just wanted someone to talk to or play with.

Now, as an adult, you think about him/her once in a while and wonder from time to time what happened to your friend who was very real to you. Did he/she disappear into nothingness when you left him/her behind to grow up in what the adults around you said was the real world? Or did your friend grow up too, in his/her own special world, in the magical world you created for him/her and you?

You decide to look inside your mind to see if he/she is still there and to discover what happened to your friend. You think that maybe, if you close your eyes and allow an image of your friend to form, you could be with him/her again, that he/she can somehow be real again.

Somewhere inside yourself, you begin to think and hope—and maybe even to believe again—that your imaginary friend might have been more than imaginary, that he/she is a special being who has the ability to magically appear in your life, just the way he/she did when you were younger.

Still believing in that magical world you enjoyed and explored as a child, you know it's always been a special part of you, and now you can remember it clearly and go there again, inside the wonder-filled world of your imagination where every thought and feeling and experience is real. Remembering the way to get there, you journey joyfully into that part of yourself you never really forgot and never truly left behind.

Calling to your friend with hopeful anticipation, you see him/her waiting for you, waiting ever so patiently for your return, waiting to embrace you again, to reunite with you and share his/her companionship and love with you.

Even though you're an adult now, your childhood friend has many special things to offer and share with you. Maybe you'll discover that he/she is all grown up now too, and that he/she has never left you, even though you may not have been aware of him/her for many years. Maybe you'll discover that your imaginary friend is really your inner child or your magical inner self.

Or maybe you'll find that your imaginary friend is just the way he/she was when you let your awareness of him/her go, and that he/she still has the magical ability to bring the child-like wonder and joy back into your life.

As you reunite with your friend and renew your bond, he/she offers you a gift, a special treasure that your soul has desired for a long time.

# Running Through the Rain

———————— ∽ ————————

*Enjoy a gentle rainfall on a warm, summer day. Be
free as a child, running joyfully through the rain.*

Watching the gentle rainfall through a window on a warm summer
day, you remember when you were a child and ran through the rain,
catching the raindrops on your tongue and tasting their delicious wet-
ness.

You remember twirling around in circles and laughing with pure
joy as the raindrops fell all around you, softly kissing your face and
skin.

You remember standing in the mud in your bare feet, squishing
the warm, gooey mud through them, feeling the softness of the earth
ooze between your toes.

You remember splashing exuberantly in the puddles on the grass
with total abandon to see how high the splashes would go.

You remember what the rain sounded like as it touched the leaves
in the trees, splattering and singing a special song to you. You remember what the sky and the clouds looked like, what the earth
smelled like, and what the wind and rain felt like on your body.

Deciding to experience all of that again, you take off your shoes,
fling open the door, and run outside to embrace and experience and
enjoy the rain in the magical way you did when you were a child.

Running joyfully through the rain, totally experiencing and enjoying your freedom and energy, you feel the wind in your hair and the gentle touch of the breeze on your body.

Turning your face up to the sky, you feel the soft kiss of the rain on your face. You feel as if you're a child again, carefree and completely happy.

# Wonderful Wishes

*Look inside your heart for your most treasured hope or desire. Make a wish upon a star and watch it magically appear in your world.*

Gazing at the clear twilight sky, you see the first star sparkling brightly in the universe. As a child, you knew that wishes were filled with magic and you remember wishing upon a star, believing that whatever you wished for would come true.

The star invites your attention and asks for your wish. There is a special hope and feeling inside you that whatever you wish for will be granted. Looking inside your mind—your heart—you think about all the wonderful things you'd like and what you would do if you had them.

Focusing on your most desired and treasured wish, you look up at the brightly-twinkling star, and you know, in a special **knowing** place inside you, that your wish will come true, if only you believe it to be so in your heart and your mind.

As you make your wish on this beautiful star in the universe, it becomes a falling star, shooting gracefully and majestically to the earth, and you know that magically, your wish is already on its way to becoming true, to being real in your physical world.

# Tapestry of Truth

*You receive an anonymous gift, a tapestry
that is woven with many colorful images,
showing an intricate design and pattern.*

You receive a special-delivery gift in the mail. The package is large and soft, wrapped in white paper, and tied with coarse threads of twine. You have no idea who sent it to you and you open it eagerly, wondering what it is.

Inside is a beautiful tapestry with many colorful images woven in and through the design. The pattern is intricate and detailed; the images are very descriptive. Looking at it more closely, you realize you're looking at a tapestry of time showing scenes that are vaguely familiar, then you begin to recognize the pattern and the images.

The tapestry reveals the pictures in your mind—the images of your thoughts, feelings, experiences, and dreams. It is a tapestry of truth, all about your life, the threads magically interwoven with the images of your life, merging the physical and spiritual worlds. One of the many things it shows you is your search for knowledge and your quest for truth.

You hang the tapestry in a special place in your home and study the images. The tapestry is timeless, showing scenes from the past, present, and future, bringing them together and blending them into the ever-present moment of here and now.

Sometimes the images are still; at other times they move. Every time you look at the tapestry, you see something new and different. It's fascinating to watch. Events seem to be happening and changing all the time, pictures appearing and disappearing, yet the design and pattern always remain interrelated and connected.

Sometimes the images blur together, as if they're occurring simultaneously. Sometimes they appear as silhouettes, echoing one another. At other times, they run side by side, paralleling and mirroring each other. Sometimes the parallels merge, sometimes they go entirely different ways.

The pictures draw you within; you're inside the images and experiencing the scenes the tapestry depicts. These events are the threads of your life, showing you the patterns and places inside your soul, intricately interwoven and filled with wonder.

As you go inside the images of this magical, mystical tapestry, you fully understand each and every experience, and each and every thought and feeling that is woven into and through the fabric of your life.

# Magical Mist

❦

*Walking in an early morning mist, you discover*
*a magical essence filled with a luminous light.*

It's early morning, just before dawn. It's light outside, yet it's a different kind of light. You notice a luminous mist that softly shrouds the earth. It looks ethereal and expansive, and you decide to go outside, walking through the softly-swirling mist.

It feels as if you are in a different world; you wonder for a moment if perhaps you're still dreaming. You feel as if you are inside a luminous light that seems to vibrate gently with energy as you feel its soft touch on your face and skin.

Walking through the early-morning mist, enjoying the feeling of complete peace and serenity, the luminous light speaks to you in your mind, in a way that your soul understands, inviting you on a magical journey as you see yourself walking through the early-morning luminous mist.

You again wonder if you're dreaming; you notice the sun is beginning to rise and the luminous mist has risen into the early morning sky, absorbing the rays of sunlight, becoming iridescent and glowing, reflecting the light within, and you feel that same glowing light within yourself.

# Spiritual Sun Ray

———————— ൴ ————————

*Explore and experience a magical, spiritual sun ray;*
*see the light of your soul reflected on the earth.*

You're in a circular clearing in a magical forest. It's still and quiet, and you feel very peaceful and spiritual here. You sense a mystical aura and ambiance in this special, sacred place within the forest that brings forth feelings of reverence inside you. You feel as if you're somewhere inside your soul rather than in a forest.

A gentle breeze caresses you and seems to touch you somewhere inside yourself. The trees all around you softly whisper through the wind to you, as if they have something of great importance to tell you—a spiritual secret. Listening to the whispers and looking around, you notice golden beams of sunlight shining through the leaves of the trees.

Standing in the center of the clearing, you look up to the sky and notice how the beams of light become brighter, sparkling and shimmering above the tops of the trees as they create intricate and interwoven patterns on the forest floor that are ever-changing in the gentle breeze. It's as if the soft touch of the wind and the light from the sun combine their essence to create the mystical ambiance all around you.

You see and sense that the wind and the light are freer and clearer above the forest. At first you think it's because there is nothing to block the flow of air or to filter the light, and, while this is true, you realize at the same time there is more to it than that. You recognize the similarity between what the universe is showing you and what you experience in your life when you go within yourself, when you look within your mind.

You see this is also true of your spiritual awareness, and that when you go above the various influences and interferences of your day-to-day activities and the physical energies of your experiences, everything is clearer and brighter, and your awareness is purer, not filtered in any way. But there is something even more special than this insight that the wind and the light have to share with you now.

The light looks warm and welcoming; it beckons to you and invites you within. As you step into a beam of light, it becomes brighter, and you feel energized and empowered. You have a sense, a knowing within you, that this light is part of you and there is a special quality you share with the light.

As the wind whispers into your mind and the ray of sunlight energizes your spirit, you somehow know, in a sacred place inside your soul, that you can travel this magical sun ray into the center of the sun.

A memory begins to open up within you that you've done this before. You also remember there is a special treasure in the center of the sun, though you can't remember exactly what it is right now. As you're standing in this beam of light, feeling its energy and power, you look at all the golden sun rays that surround you, and the memory begins to become clear in your mind.

You remember the treasure is the light of your soul that opens up your spiritual knowledge, and that this gift is given to all souls and is meant for sharing. You know that all you have to do to receive and open this gift is to know it is already yours; it is your spiritual birthright. Looking upward, you begin to travel through the light of the sun ray into the sun, flying high above the earth into the universe, into the center of the sun.

As the spirit of the sun gives you your special gift—the light of your soul, your inner truth, and the complete remembrance of all your spiritual knowledge—she tells you that the sunrise every morning is your reminder to open your gift and radiate your light everywhere, every day, in and through all your experiences, and to share it with other souls.

Traveling within the sun ray—your special essence of light—joyfully sharing the gift you have received from the sun—the gift you've given to yourself from your soul, your inner light begins to grow brighter and to radiate with its own sacred, unique light to illuminate the world.

You notice you're now over the clearing in the forest where you began your journey. Floating down gently through the tops of the trees, you land softly back on the earth, knowing that the sun—the universal essence of light—is the most special and sacred place you have ever seen, the most wondrous place you have ever been, and that your soul has just taken a brief journey home to remember and renew its essence.

You are a special, spiritual sun ray, and you recognize that the sacred gift you received—the treasure you've always known is within you—is the inner light of your soul, emanating and radiating everywhere, shining brightly upon the earth, filling the world and the universe with love, peace, joy, and harmony.

Let your light shine brightly.

# Guardian Angel

*See the special friend who has been with you all your life. Recognize the many times he or she has appeared in your life and the many ways your angel has helped, guided, and protected you.*

A radiant being appears before you in a glowing ball of light that sparkles and shimmers with the ethereal essence of the universe. Stepping out of the light, you immediately recognize this beautiful being as the guardian angel who has always been with you in every moment of your life.

She* reaches forward to touch you, to embrace and hold you lovingly. As you move toward her and feel her tender touch, you are deeply moved by a very joyful emotion that words cannot describe.

You feel the love and joy that emanates from her and surrounds you completely, filling you with a warmth that soothes your soul and calms your mind.

Closing your eyes, you see and remember the many times and ways, and magical moments, your guardian angel has appeared to you and been with you, and all the ways she has helped, guided, and protected you. Very often she has spoken to you in your thoughts and created beautiful images as she danced through your dreams in sparkles and shimmers of light.

Reflecting on the many times she has appeared in your life, you see that she has taken many forms, some seen and some unseen. At times, she may have appeared as a person who offered you a word of kindness or encouragement. At other times you may have seen her as a beautiful flower that caught your attention and brought you joy.

You may have sensed her presence in a beautiful rainbow that inspired a sense of awe and wonder and joy inside you. You may have felt her presence as a gentle whisper of the wind softly caressing your face, a wonderful feeling of warmth and love, a gentle wave of energy vibrating around you, or a protective force that kept you safe from impending harm or danger.

You may have physically felt a soft kiss on your cheek, a gentle brush on your shoulder, or a touch of healing to ease an ache or a pain. You may have heard her voice when she softly spoke to you, calling your name when no one was there, or you may have heard music—sounds of your soul played by her.

She may have been in the light of a person's eyes when they smiled at you. You may have seen her in a sparkle of light just beyond the periphery of your vision or in a star that twinkled at you from the universe.

See the times she has appeared in your thoughts and dreams. See her in your intuition and insight when perhaps she offered an idea or an answer to a question, helped you find a solution to a problem, gave you direction and guidance when you were troubled, or helped you find your way when you were lost.

Remember the times, inside your feelings and emotions, when she soothed you when you were sad, or cheered you up with a thought or a feeling of love that seemed to come from out of nowhere. Remember when she brought you feelings of peace and harmony when you most needed them, and when she shared very special moments of joy with you.

Think about the many times she has played inside your imagination, drifting magically through your daydreams and floating in your reveries, offering you light-heartedness, happiness, and joy. Remember the times she has given you very special gifts that were either tangible or intangible—ones that may have been of a physical or a spiritual nature.

Renew your deep and abiding relationship with her, knowing your guardian angel has always been there for you and that she will always be in your life, in both the magical and the mundane moments.

*Angels can also be male or androgynous, or an ethereal essence. For purposes of clarity in this meditation, your guardian angel has been referred to as female.

# Healing Nourishment

*Experience healing and renewal as you enjoy a
special healing rain which nourishes and blesses you
with abundant health in body, mind, and spirit.*

You have a wonderful, sacred ability within yourself for healing and renewal.

Imagine you're walking outside on a pleasantly warm summer day, enjoying the light of the sunshine. You feel the warmth gently permeating your skin; you feel as if you're absorbing the light within yourself.

You feel a wonderful sense of peace and harmony within you. You're completely enjoying being outside and breathing in the pure, clean air on this beautiful day that is filled with light. You notice a few puffy white clouds that are filled with light, gently floating in the sky above you. You notice how they absorb the rays of light from the sun and how they reflect the light of the sun.

You know these clouds are very special because they are filled with liquid drops of healing light. As the rain softly begins to fall, you notice how the rain caresses and cleanses the earth, healing and rejuvenating it. You listen to the gentle patter of the rain on the leaves of the trees and notice how the raindrops cling to the leaves, nourishing and renewing them.

You're completely enjoying this experience of walking in this very special healing rain. The rain feels like warm, gentle kisses on your skin. You feel the light rain gently nourishing and healing you as it softly touches your skin. The soft, gentle raindrops somehow seem to enter inside you—inside your body, circulating through you, cleansing and healing you from the inside out.

Even as the rain continues to gently fall, the light from the sun emerges, showering the earth with light, and a shimmering rainbow appears. You feel the awe and wonder and beauty of it inside your heart and soul. Looking around you at the wet, beautiful earth, you notice all the sparkling rainbows dancing on the leaves of the bushes and the petals of the flowers that are opening up to the light.

Breathing in deeply, you smell the wonderful scent of the wet earth, freshly nourished and cleansed by the rain. As you tune into all these wondrous things around you, and bring them inside you, you feel the joy and harmony of them within your heart.

The earth and the universe have just blessed you with a beautiful gift—a shower of cleansing, healing rain for your spirit that washed your heart, refreshed your mind, and bathed your soul. You feel a wonderful sense of being nourished and completely healed in body, mind, and spirit by this beautiful rainfall of liquid light.

# Releasing a Request

———————— ❧ ————————

*You have a very special request, a hope you'd like
to see realized, or a dream you'd like to have come
true, or a question you'd like to have answered,
or perhaps a problem you'd like to have solved.*

Think about your special request very carefully and in great detail. Ponder all the reasons why you want it and how you'll feel when it is granted. See what you will do with it when you receive it, and how you will share it.

Imagine all the things that may need to occur in your life before your request is granted. See those things happening in your mind and be open to receiving other ideas, insights, and images that show you things you may not have thought of or considered yet.

Feel a wonderful sense of hope in your heart, and believe that your request is manifesting even as you think about it. Be loving in your desire and appreciative in your anticipation. Simply feel the joy of it in your soul.

Begin to put your thoughts, feelings, insights, ideas, and images into motion by taking action on them to bring them into being. Be spontaneous and free with your actions, going with the flow of them, listening to your inner thoughts and following your feelings. Trust and know that your request will come to be, yet remain detached from achieving specific results so that even better things can occur.

As you prepare to receive the fulfillment of your request, you may decide to also ask for help from higher sources so that whatever happens will be the most beneficial for everyone who is involved or who will be touched by it.

In your mind, write your request on a piece of paper, pouring out all your thoughts and feelings about it. Give the paper to a beautiful white dove who is waiting on the sill of an open window.

As the dove flies into the universe with your request, you know it is being fulfilled in the proper timing and in the most appropriate manner for the highest good of all.

# Walking Through the Woods

—————————— ✑ ——————————

*Journey into a special forest and listen to
the wisdom of a tree that shares the secrets of
the earth and the knowledge of the universe.*

Imagine a very pleasant, warm summer day. You decide to go for a walk through the woods to renew your relationship with nature and to reconnect with the earth—to appreciate its beauty and to experience the joy and harmony of the earth with the universe. Deep inside yourself, you know you're part of that special connection and you'd like to feel that again.

The day is filled with the quiet sounds of nature; you feel and hear the gentle breeze as it touches you and moves softly through the leaves of the trees in the forest you see ahead of you. Walking toward the trees, you feel the warmth of the sun and begin to re-experience the sense of aliveness and vibrancy that being in nature brings you.

Breathing in deeply, you feel the pure, clean air circulate through your lungs, revitalizing and rejuvenating every part of your mind and your body. As this energy flows through your body, you feel lighter and happier. As it flows through your mind, all your cares and worries slip away as you enjoy this beautiful day, this wonderful walk through nature.

Entering the forest, you notice how the sunshine sparkles through the tops of the trees, creating shafts and streams of light from the sky to the earth, and you see how the breeze interacts with the leaves and plays with patterns on the forest floor. You notice how intricate the patterns are, and how they're constantly moving and changing.

Walking through the open, airy forest, you notice how quiet it is inside the forest and how peaceful it is. You begin to enter a meditative frame of mind, a special, serene place within yourself where you feel completely comfortable and natural.

You see a tall, majestic tree in the center of a clearing up ahead. The sunlight sparkles and shimmers all around the tree as it beckons you forth, inviting you forward and welcoming you as if you are an old and very dear friend. You know you've been here before—in your thoughts and in your dreams.

Feeling perfectly at home and in tune with yourself, you walk slowly, thoughtfully, into the clearing. Sitting quietly on the soft ground next to the tree, enjoying the feeling of peace and harmony within you and all around you, you begin to remember.

The gentle breeze creates a light, musical sound that vibrates in harmony within your mind as the wind blows softly through the leaves of the tree. Leaning up against the tree, you listen to your thoughts and watch their images move in your mind.

The leaves whisper in the wind, sharing the secrets of nature and the knowledge of the universe. Somehow you know you can communicate with the tree, and you listen as it tells you about its connection with the earth and the universe, about how its roots are connected to the earth as its branches reach toward the sky, toward the universe.

The tree speaks to you of the harmony that is within nature, the harmony the earth and the universe share, and the harmony you share between your physical self and your spiritual self. It tells you the universe is within you and that you are the universe, expressing your spiritual nature—your true self—in earthly form. As you listen and remember, you begin to reunite with yourself, joining your physical awareness with your spiritual essence, feeling all the joy and harmony this brings within you.

Looking up at the sky, you see a few puffy white clouds floating by, and you notice how blue and expansive the sky is. It seems to go on forever, beyond the horizon into the universe and even farther than that into infinity.

The sky has an ethereal quality—a magical, mystical essence you know within your mind, yet can't describe with words—a majesty you've known before but haven't experienced for a while. Breathing in deeply, you absorb the depth of the blueness within yourself; the color fills you with a wonderful feeling of peace and awareness, with a deep inner sense of remembrance and knowing.

Standing up, you feel as if you could reach up through the sky and touch the universe. Stretching your arms upward in an open embrace toward the sky, you feel a magical surge of energy and power inside you, knowing you're part of the earth and the universe; that you're in harmony with the physical world around you and the spiritual world within you.

You sense how infinite those worlds really are and you begin to remember how infinite you really are. You become fully aware of how awesome the world really is, and you rediscover how awesome you really are; you fully sense your true spiritual nature, and the knowledge and power of the universe, completely opening up and expanding within you.

You decide to continue walking, to explore everything you see, and to experience and understand both the world within you and the world around you.

Reaching the edge of the forest, you turn and look back, knowing you've just taken a wonderful walk through the woods. You've remembered the truth of your spiritual nature and reunited with yourself as the tree shared its true nature and its treasures of knowledge with you. You've reconnected with the earth and re-experienced the joy and harmony of the earth with the universe—the harmony of your physical self with your spiritual self.

As you continue forward in your life, carry with you the special knowledge that you're truly a spiritual being, and you are connected in a very special way with both the earth and the universe.

# Travels of Time

―――――――――― ∽ ――――――――――

*Somewhere in your journeys, you meet an old spiritual master who shares a few secrets and surprises with you.*

You find yourself walking with a spiritual guide or a master in a universal dimension of energy and awareness. As you talk and walk together, you begin to recognize this being as a very special friend—or perhaps he or she is your higher self—that you've traveled with many times before, seeking and sharing knowledge. As you open the vibrations of your soul, you remember.

In this self-guided meditation, draw an image and a feeling of walking with a very knowledgeable master, one with whom you come to realize and recognize is an old friend.

Perhaps at first you thought this master was the teacher and you were the student, but as you talk and walk together, you become aware the two of you are equals, and can both share your knowledge with one another. Travel with this person to find your truth.

When you are done, for the moment, with this meditation, reflect on the inner journey you've just taken into the spiritual realms of yourself as you traveled within and with your soul. You know all of life is an inner journey and that your soul shines a light on your path, showing you the way home to your true spiritual nature.

# Waterfall of Light

—————————— ℘ ——————————

*Experience a shimmering, sparkling waterfall of*
*light that invites you to bathe in its healing energies,*
*refreshing and rejuvenating you in body, mind, and spirit.*

You're in a beautiful, peaceful place in nature that is serene and quiet, covered with the most beautiful green grass you've ever seen or felt under your feet. You notice a tall oak tree next to a calm, reflecting pond.

You see how the shadows of the leaves interplay on the surface of the water. You notice the shadows of the leaves cover only half the pond. The other half shimmers with sunlight that creates sparkling patterns on the surface of the pond.

You feel a gentle breeze caress you softly and watch the water as it responds to the breeze by creating gentle ripples on its surface as it simultaneously creates a soft musical sound in your mind, like harmonious wind chimes.

You know you're in a magical place, and that this pond is very special; you know it has a spiritual purpose. Walking closer to the edge of the water, you notice the pond reflects the shadows of the leaves, just as it reflects the sparkles of sunlight, and it also reflects your thoughts and feelings. The sunlight mirrors all the positive, loving thoughts and feelings you have inside your soul; the shadows echo your negative thoughts, feelings, doubts, worries, and fears.

Walking around the pond, you see there is a place where all the shadows disappear, where the water is clear and sparkling. You know that viewing the pond from this perspective gives you an entirely new perception of it. You know the shadows are only there if you see that they are there.

As you look at the water in this calm reflecting pond, you know you can place all your thoughts there and they will be reflected back to you in the motion of a soft breeze that creates gentle ripples on the surface of the water.

You're drawn to the sparkling, shimmering side of the pond that reflects your soul. And yet you know, you sense, there is a positive purpose for the shadows, though you can no longer see them from your current viewpoint.

The water looks inviting, and you know it is absolutely pure in nature. You decide to dip your hand into the clear pool of water, wanting a cool, refreshing drink. As you bend down to touch the water, it rises up to you in a magical fountain for you to drink from. You drink deeply from the pure spring of water, knowing you are drinking in its magical qualities, its healing essence, the purity of your soul.

You decide you'd like to splash the water on your face, to feel its wonderful coolness and serenity, to feel its magical aura around you. The water sprinkles you with a gentle spray on your face, returning to the pond in soft shimmers and sparkles of sunlight.

The water you drank and the gentle spray you felt on your face has had a wonderful, rejuvenating effect on you. You feel much happier and lighter than you did before you came to this magical place. A feeling of joy comes over you, and you want to experience all the magic this wonderful pond has to give you, all the magic your soul has to give you.

You decide you'd like to bathe in the water, to bathe in the essence of your soul. At the very moment you think the thought, the water rises up in the center, creating a very beautiful waterfall in a rhythm of motion with harmonious, beautiful sounds, radiating and reflecting sparkles and shimmers of light, echoing the light of your soul.

You look at the waterfall that is shimmering and sparkling with light, knowing it will be as refreshing and magical as the water you drank and the water that sprayed your face. You notice there is something different about the waterfall that came from the water in the pond.

It shimmers and sparkles in the same manner as the sunlight that was reflected on the surface of the gently rippling water, but the waterfall is not composed of water; it is composed of light. Beautiful, warm, inviting sprays and showers of sparkling, shimmering light. Somehow, magically, the water has changed into vibrations of light. You wonder if your thoughts and feelings had anything to do with it.

Reflecting on your thoughts and feelings, you realize you were drawn to this side of the pond by the sparkles and shimmers of sunlight that played on the surface, creating a magical melody that sang to your soul as the soft breeze gently caressed you and created a gentle movement on the water.

You step into the waterfall of light, wanting to completely experience it with every part of you, wanting to be completely in tune with it, wanting to be completely in tune with your soul. A feeling of total harmony and complete, perfect peace washes over you and bathes you in a waterfall of light, gently permeating every pore of your body, then circulating and flowing through you—through your body, mind, and spirit—filling your entire being with that same perfect peace and harmony.

You are completely immersed in this wonderful, beautiful, magical, healing waterfall of light. The light is effervescent and bubbly; it's like bathing in gentle bubbles of energy. The light gives you a wonderful feeling of being totally alive and completely healthy.

The light feels exhilarating, soothing, and peaceful at the same time as it nourishes and nurtures you, as it cleanses you in body, mind, and spirit, revitalizing and rejuvenating every part of you, as it showers you with health and harmony, peace and joy, as it washes you completely in the vibrations of your soul.

You step out of the pond, out of the waterfall of your soul's light that was so nourishing and rejuvenating, the light that filled you so completely with health, harmony, and happiness. The waterfall returns to the pond, shimmering with sunlight again.

Stepping back from the pond, you see the shadows of the leaves again, but this time you understand and know why they are there. The waterfall of light has gently and completely drawn from you all your cares, worries, problems, ailments, and negative thoughts, washing them away from you and giving them to the shadows of the leaves, replacing them with beautiful, radiant health and happiness inside you.

You see the pond in a new way, with a clearer vision. Even as you watch the shadows on the pond, the gentle music of the breeze blows them away, letting the light shine through as it disperses all the shadows, so the pond reflects your vibrant health, your positive thoughts and feelings, and the essence of your soul.

You know you can return to this magical pond of healing at any time you choose. It will always be there because the waterfall of light is a reflection of your true spiritual nature.

# Multidimensional Meadow

———————————— ❦ ————————————

*In a multidimensional meadow, filled with flowers
dancing in a gentle breeze, you discover beings of light
who share the essence of light and shower you with joy.*

It's a pleasantly warm, sunny day with a gentle breeze. You see beautiful, colorful flowers growing wild and free in an open, expansive meadow. Slowly walking among the flowers, you see the sunlight shimmering all around them. The light also seems to come from within them. You sense how truly alive the flowers are; you sense how special and magical they are; growing in perfect harmony with the earth and the universe.

The meadow seems to vibrate with a special sense of energy that resonates with your soul. The soft, luxuriant green grass feels like velvet beneath your feet. The sun feels warm and pleasant on your face as it touches you with light.

The meadow is filled with thousands, perhaps millions of colorful, vibrant flowers. The flowers seem to go on forever, as far as your eyes can see. Each flower sparkles with light as it shares its wonderful fragrance.

The harmony of the scene calls to you, inviting you to explore further. You feel your soul being drawn into the meadow. Looking at the flowers, you see that light flickers softly in the center of each flower. Breathing in their wonderful fragrance, you sense their inner essence and become aware of how they're connected to both the earth and the universe, just as you are. You become aware of their natural harmony with the world around them and the world within them, just as you sense and experience the natural harmony of your physical self with your spiritual self.

The flowers are vibrantly alive, flowing with the natural energy and harmony of life and their inner essence, and you know you're even more vibrantly alive, flowing with the energy of life and the essence of your spirituality.

You completely sense and absorb the colors and fragrances, and the energies of the flowers within you, and—in a way you somehow completely understand—you become the colors, you become the flowers, you become the fragrance, you become one with their essence.

A flower seems to call to you. Walking over to it and touching it lovingly and gently, you notice it's a bud just beginning to open up, just as your spiritual awareness is opening up. You watch as the flower continues to open up, petal by petal, as your awareness continues to open up, to grow and bloom and blossom into inner wisdom and knowledge, into the realness of inner knowing and spiritual awareness.

You sit down on the soft green grass in the meadow, wanting to commune with the flowers, with all of nature. You feel completely in tune with nature all around you. As you're sitting amidst the flowers, admiring and appreciating their gentle beauty and quiet serenity, and the vibrations of peace and harmony they're offering and sharing with you, you hear a soft whisper in your mind and realize it's also in the air and all around you.

Listening, you pinpoint the source of the sound, and notice it's coming from a flower—that the flower is talking to you; that all the flowers are talking to one another, communicating in their special way. You realize you're in a magical meadow where you can hear and communicate with the world of nature, where you can talk to and listen to the flowers, and understand their language.

You remember that, as a child, you would often talk to the flowers and listen to them as they spoke to you. Looking at the flower that spoke to you now, you see a little ray of light emanating and sparkling from the center of it. At first you think it's a reflection of sunlight glistening from a small drop of nectar in its center. Looking closely at the flower, you recognize it looks more like a flower fairy, reminiscent of fairies you've seen in a garden before.

You smile to yourself, then laugh with pure joy and happiness. The flower fairies you used to believe in when you were a child are **real**. You remember how you used to play with the fairies who were your friends, how you used to dance and sing and laugh with them.

As you grew up, you placed this wonder-filled time in your memory as a magical game of make-believe, but deep inside you knew it was much more than pretend, and you kept this memory in a special place inside your mind.

You wonder why you're experiencing this now, then you know. You want to be in that magical world that is vibrantly alive, waiting only for you to fully remember and recognize it—to open your mind and soul, and become aware of it again.

You know this meadow is more than a special, magical place in your mind—a wonderful memory reopening. You know this multidimensional meadow exists in both worlds—the world within of your spiritual knowing and the world of nature around you of your physical consciousness.

As this awareness opens up inside you, the multidimensional meadow expands in the light—transforming and growing into a garden—and you're standing at the entrance to the most beautiful garden you've ever seen or been in before. The garden is flowing out and expanding from the meadow into what seems like infinity from where you're standing.

A softly-swirling mist surrounds the meadow, or perhaps it's sunbeams—rays of light—and they only appear to be misty because of the clouds floating above the meadow. You know you're ready to see through the mist, into the clear light of your soul.

The scene is enchanting, like something out of a movie and yet you know it's very real. You sense it's a special, sacred place where you can become even more aware of your true essence—your real self. You feel a soft breeze flowing through this garden, gently caressing you.

Rays of light shine through the mist as it begins to clear. The sunlight shimmers all around you as you look at this garden filled with shimmering, iridescent butterflies, floating joyfully on the soft breeze. Your spirit feels free and happy, loving how free the butterflies are and how joyful they seem to be, playing with the flowers and floating on the breeze.

The meadow glows with a shimmering light, vibrating with a special, sacred energy. Everything seems ethereal and transparent, even though it looks solid at the same time. The meadow is multidimensional, forming and reforming itself in every moment. You realize nothing is really as it appears to be.

A gentle wind is blowing, as soft as a whisper. You watch as the flowers dance in harmony with the gentle breeze—radiating sparkles and shimmers of light. You take a few steps forward, feeling a sense of awe and reverence inside you. The flowers seem to be whispering to one another as they dance in the gentle breeze that shimmers with light. The whispers are welcoming you into the garden.

You walk into the whispers of light in the garden. Looking closer at the flowers, you see a sparkle in the center of each one. You wonder if the flowers here are also tended by the flower fairies—the ones you communicated with earlier. You remember how they whispered to you when you touched the flowers.

Looking closer, you see something very different about them. The sparkle of light looks like little butterflies, with multicolored wings of light. When one lands on a flower, the petals open up, radiating colors of light all around the flower and the butterfly who is tending the flower, spreading happiness and joy.

Or perhaps the butterfly's wings create the shimmering light, and the flowers respond to the soft whispers of light by opening up to receive the joyful expression of the light. It seems the light from the butterfly's wings create the beautiful scent of the flowers as they dance among them.

You look around at all the beautiful flowers. It seems that joy fills each flower that is dancing in the gentle breeze, radiating vibrations of happiness and laughter as the butterfly's wings whisper, softly touching each flower, their rainbow auras merging into brilliant, ever-changing colors of light.

The butterflies are also whispering to you, filling you with joy and light as they welcome you and dance around you. You feel as if you're a flower, filled with light, dancing with the rainbow butterflies as they shimmer above you.

# Star Dancing

*Dance among the stars, weaving together the threads of
ethereal light and universal energies into your experiences.*

Free your spirit from being earth-bound. You know you can travel
above the earth through threads of light from the universe. You're a
physical being, but more importantly, you're a spiritual being. You're
part of the universe.

You can take your consciousness above the earth reality and
dance in and among the stars, weaving your dreams into the fabric of
the universe and spinning your essence through the light.

Imagine a brilliant night sky, lit up with thousands of stars in the
universe that sparkle and shimmer with light. Looking up, you know
your soul is part of the universe, a star filled with light. With that
thought, you rise into the sky.

Dancing among the stars, through the vibrations of ethereal light
in the universe, you notice that every time you move, you emanate
and radiate sparkles of light, weaving the threads of your energy and
your essence.

You see threads of light that emanate from you, from the star that
is you, joining together in perfect harmony and synchronicity with

every star in the universe, sharing light and energy, sharing a dance of harmony.

Dancing through the universe, exploring and expanding your light and energy, you weave together your dreams with ethereal threads of light, creating beautiful patterns inside your soul that vibrate in tune with your physical experiences.

Your dance inspires the movement of the threads of energies, through infinite vibrations and variations of all your experiences, as you flow through the motions of the universe and the rhythms of your soul, shining your light upon the earth.

Looking at the earth, you recognize that the light of your soul shines through your energy essence on earth, emanating and radiating sparkles of universal light with and through and in every thought, feeling, and experience you have.

You return to yourself on earth, knowing you are the essence of universal light. Looking up at the stars again, you know the dreams you've woven into the fabric of the universe are the dreams that are woven into your heart from your soul.

# Moonbeam Magic

— ❡ —

*Ride a moonbeam into the universe and*
*explore the infinite reaches of your mind.*

Looking up at the starry night with a luminous full moon, you see the aura around the moon and rays of light emanating and radiating from the moon and the stars, reflecting the light of the universe. The rays of light appear to be moonbeams of magic sparkling and shimmering with an ethereal energy essence, as if they are calling to you.

You feel as if you could magically travel a moonbeam into the universe. You've been on an inner journey for a while now, and you know this is entirely possible.

You think about the path you're traveling in your quest for knowledge to find the truth within yourself. You want to know the infinite awareness of your mind and the vastness of your spiritual knowledge, and the universe seems to be the perfect place to expand your self-discovery.

You decide to travel a moonbeam into the universe, to explore the infinite reaches of your mind, and to experience and know the mysteries of your soul. With that thought, you find yourself riding on a moonbeam of light, going into the universe and beyond, exploring the openness of your mind and the expansiveness of your soul.

# Part Three

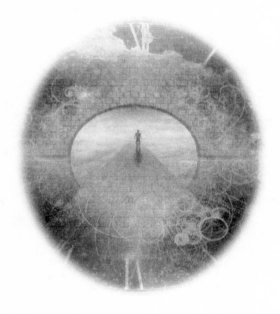

*Mystical Meditations*

**Part Three** centers on the theme of remembering your spiritual knowledge and reawakening your spiritual self. The meditations offer spiritual journeys that invite you to tune into the essence of your soul.

Once upon a time, somewhere inside your soul, you knew everything there was to know. These meditations help you remember what you've always known and how to bring it forth in your life to show you the wonder-filled magic you have within your soul.

They illuminate the journeys of your spirit to see the light of your soul reflected within yourself and mirrored all around you as they invite you to travel on the gentle, peaceful wings of your spirit. As the meditations move gently through your thoughts and step softly through your soul, you'll see your mind opening up and expanding into ever-widening and broader horizons, and you'll experience your soul stretching to new heights of awareness and enlightenment.

These meditations invite you to travel further than the center of yourself and deeper within to the very core of your being, to touch and fully experience your essence, to journey above and beyond yourself into your true spiritual nature, into the multidimensionality of your soul. They hold the promise of growing your soul, if you will look into your mind to recognize the light within you, and see into your soul to remember who you truly are—a powerful, spiritual being of light.

# Spiritual Storyteller

***

*Gather around an old storyteller in a*
*park and listen to the stories he tells you.*

You notice a group of people gathered around someone in a park. Interested in what is going on, you join the crowd and work your way up to the front. There you see an old man who is telling stories, wonderful parables and proverbs that inspire musings and messages as they create images and draw symbols that form into moving pictures in your mind.

He's very eloquent and articulate. As his words weave around you, entering into your imagination and through your awareness, they spin into meanings that at first you may barely comprehend with your conscious mind, but somewhere inside you, you understand. You know.

Listening to his magical, mystical stories, and allowing them to take you into a special world of knowing within yourself, you begin to recognize the metaphysical meanings in the words he speaks.

You listen more attentively, focusing on his words, hearing with your mind as he speaks, elucidating the knowing that is already within you, helping you recognize and remember your own spiritual knowledge. His words weave a tapestry of truth, magically blending the physical and the spiritual worlds, bringing them together. You realize you're listening to a master storyteller—a true teacher.

Inspired and intrigued by the stories he tells, you want to learn so much more. It seems he knows everything there is to know about everything. It appears he is speaking directly to you now, somehow knowing what's inside your heart, what you need to hear, and the answers you seek.

At times, he becomes quiet. While you may think it's because he's gathering his thoughts, it's because he wisely knows that silence holds your answers, and he wants you to look within yourself for the truth. As you listen within, you begin to hear your own inner voice in the silence that blends with his as it becomes your voice you're listening to.

You become aware that you're hearing the stories of your own spiritual knowing, and that this spiritual storyteller is your inner storyteller, your spiritual self, at first whispering softly to you in your thoughts, feelings, and dreams, then the more you listen, the more you hear and the more you become aware of and know.

# A Gift From the Gods

*You're given a gift from the gods, a
treasure more priceless and valuable than
any other the physical world has to offer.*

You hear a soft, whooshing sound above you as a white gift box tied
with a purple ribbon falls from the sky, landing softly beside you.
Picking it up, thinking it's a gift from the universe, you wonder
what's inside.

Opening the gift box, you see that it appears to be empty, but as
you peer closer, you notice a shimmer of light and a small, slim book
appears, seemingly from out of nowhere. Somehow you know this
book is the story of your soul. Opening the book, eager to read it, you
notice the pages are blank, but you're determined to decode the messages you know are written there.

Flipping through the pages, you begin to see faint, barely visible
images of words. As you read the word-images, they become moving
pictures that begin to fill in with colors and details; they become more
vivid and descriptive the more you place your attention and awareness on them.

The pictures tell you the story of your life and show you the many
different experiences of your soul. With every page you turn, the
book grows in volume and size as more pages are added, showing
you the many different aspects of your soul, and the many avenues

and directions your soul has traveled—the paths it has followed and the journeys it has taken.

It seems as if the book is writing itself as you read it, but you know you have the power to edit and revise this book, to write and rewrite it any way you choose to. It is both fiction and nonfiction, containing all the facts and the many faces and facets of your soul. It describes—in vibrant, illuminating images and words—the dearest and most private wishes and hopes in your heart. It offers you stories, parables, and proverbs—some symbolic and some literal.

This book of knowledge shows you many insights into your soul as it offers you images of journeys you've taken and glimpses of journeys your soul will travel in the future. It contains possibilities and probabilities, and shares with you various imprints of experiences yet to be as it offers you choices as to how you'd like to shape and sculpt the future.

It invites you to listen to your thoughts and feelings, and to look within your mind, heart, and soul—into your imagination to write and rewrite the past, present, and future—to change your feelings and experiences with a slight stroke of your thoughts and a soft touch of your emotions.

This magical, mystical book is a gift from the gods—a treasure of truth—given to you to open and read your spiritual knowledge, your inner knowing, and to write the story of your soul.

# Energy Essence

⤜ ∾ ⤛

*In a sacred place inside your soul,*
*you remember who you really are.*

You feel as if you're wandering through a softly-swirling misty maze—a shimmering space—in search of something special within you. It's just a vague feeling at the moment, and you're not quite sure what you're looking for, but know you'll recognize it immediately when you find it.

You feel as if you're on a journey in search of your soul, looking for your spiritual knowledge and your true spiritual essence.

Perhaps you're looking for the meaning and purpose in your life, or a special knowing somewhere inside your soul. It feels as if something is missing or misplaced, yet you know you can find it; you can remember it.

You feel as if you're on a wonderful adventure that will either lead you onto the path you've chosen to follow or will show you the way to continue on the path you already journey upon.

You begin to look inside your mind, peering into almost-forgotten dreams and misty memories, searching for an image, a clue, a doorway, or a window—a way to remember. You begin to get clearer on what you're searching for.

What you're looking for is the answer to something you've pondered and puzzled over for many years, perhaps many lifetimes. You

want to know who you really are and why you are here. You're looking for the realness in life, for the meaning and purpose, and for what
you are meant to do with your life.

But you know it goes much deeper than that. You realize you're
looking for your spiritual essence, for the knowledge and truth inside
you. You want to reconnect with your spiritual self, to see through
the earthly illusions you've enshrouded yourself in. You want to see
through your physical nature into the true reality of your spiritual nature. You're looking for yourself—your soul.

You quiet your conscious mind and go within the stillness of
yourself, knowing the answers you seek are there. An image and a
thought sparkles into your awareness and suddenly you know. Your
answer appears as if by magic, and you laugh with the pure joy and
exhilaration of finding something you've always known but have
temporarily forgotten.

In a sacred place inside your soul, you remember who you really
are and why you are here now. You remember your soul's purpose.
With this remembrance comes the complete awareness of your true
spiritual nature, and you reunite with yourself, gently wrapping the
essence of your soul around you.

It feels as if you are being embraced with the gentleness and love
and joy of your true spiritual self, as if you are coming home. You
know you've found yourself and that you have given yourself a very
special gift. You've found what you've been searching for—your
true spiritual nature.

At the same time, you remember all your spiritual knowledge.
With this awareness, you know you can fully express the pure energy
of your soul and share your spiritual knowledge in every moment, as
the essence of your soul is mirrored and reflected in every emotion
and experience in your life.

# Setting Your Spirit Free

꙰

*Watch the birth of a butterfly as it emerges from
its golden chrysalis; see through physical boundaries
into the unlimited potential and knowledge of your
soul as you open your wings to fly and expand
your awareness into your spiritual essence.*

Walking in a magical field, listening to your thoughts, you know your
true nature is that of a free spirit, dressed in a physical body. Your
soul isn't limited in any way by physical energies, and you know you
can expand your awareness and transcend the limits and restrictions
of physical energies.

You know your soul vibrates to spiritual and universal energies,
in tune with nature and the universe, moving in rhythm with knowledge and awareness, in harmony with light. Your soul is the universal energy of light, and you know you can feel and experience your
spirit in its pure energy form.

Listening to your thoughts, you compare your soul to a butterfly
that's free, moving on wings of spiritual and universal energies. You
know you can unwrap the physical cocoon of earthly energies and
break through the paper-like shell of limited consciousness to open
up your awareness and set your spirit free.

A movement in a nearby bush catches your attention. You see a
beautiful butterfly emerging from its golden chrysalis. Watching its
birth, you realize you're seeing something very special and magical.

The butterfly has just emerged into the light and is beginning to open its wings to fly, to explore its new life as a transformed being— as a free spirit. As the butterfly spreads its wings, they shimmer in the sunlight and you realize that, in essence, you are very much like the butterfly.

You feel at one with it and in harmony with the world around you and within you. You begin to understand what the butterfly feels like as it frees itself and begins to fly, floating on gentle currents of air, enjoying the light of the sunshine all around it, rising and soaring into the sky and through the clouds.

You feel as if you could rise and soar with the butterfly, in harmony with air and light. You feel as if you could rise and soar into the universe, transcending physical boundaries and limits, moving upward through the clouds into the light of your spiritual energies. You feel as if you could rise even higher into universal energies, where your soul is open and free in its true form.

Becoming more in tune with the energies of the butterfly—with the energies of your spiritual nature—you feel as if you are the butterfly, and you understand its natural harmony with the earth and the universe. Simultaneously you become aware of your natural harmony with the earth and the universe; you become aware that you can transcend earthly energies and flow into universal energies of awareness and light.

You begin to feel yourself opening up and expanding through the energies of your physical reality, transforming yourself into the vibrations of your spiritual self. Blending into your spiritual awareness, you begin to feel even more open and expansive and free, much as you imagine the butterfly felt when it peered through and released itself from its transparent, paper-like cocoon.

Flowing and floating upward into higher vibrations of awareness and light, you become in tune with your spiritual energies and you feel the essence of your soul. You feel as if you could fly on wings of light.

You feel the freeness and naturalness of your inner spirit, taking wing and flying through the air, into the azure-blue sky of the universe. As you experience this, you feel yourself—your awareness—blending into the energies of the universe, in harmony with the earth.

As the butterfly continues to float and fly, you feel yourself floating even higher, traveling on the iridescent, shimmering wings of your spirit, emerging and expanding into knowledge and light. The butterfly is free—flying, soaring above the earth—and you feel just as free. You're free of the clouds of physical energies; you've emerged into the energy of your soul.

You feel your spirit begin to fly and soar and expand into ever-higher realms and realities of knowledge and awareness and light. Flying and soaring upward, higher and higher, you feel the freedom of knowledge and the light of awareness. Floating on natural currents of air and energy, you feel your spirit becoming more and more free.

As you continue to rise into the true awareness of your spirit, you see sparkles of light—rays of sunshine and the radiance of stars—that illuminate the sky. They feel vibrant and peaceful and nourishing as they shower you with awareness, as they shower the earth with light.

Absorbing the light and energy, you feel very vibrant and peaceful and nourished from the universe and from within yourself, knowing you're really a free spirit, and that you're experiencing the energies of the true nature of your soul. You feel illuminated with the energy of the universe, with the light of sunshine and the vibrant radiance of the stars—with the energy of your inner knowing and the light of your spiritual awareness.

You continue to fly and soar upward, higher and higher, becoming more and more free—transcending the earthly pull of physical energies, expanding into ever-widening horizons of true knowledge and awareness—flying on wings of illumination and light.

Your spirit is free, flying and soaring and expanding into the universe, moving with the motion and rhythm of knowledge and awareness and light.

# Stairway to Spirituality

———————— ଓ ————————

*Ascend into the universe, traveling the*
*22 steps to spirituality that lead you into*
*your soul's evolvement and enlightenment.*

You're high on a massive mountain, standing in a beautiful green grassy area. Looking all around, you see a few tall trees in the distance that reach up into the sky. Beyond the trees, there is a huge boulder that seems to encompass almost the entire top of the mountain as it rises up into the misty, ethereal clouds.

Being an adventuresome soul, you're more than a little curious about what is behind the boulder, what is hidden from you. You wonder what you'd find if you were able to travel to the top of it, to see beyond it into the universe. You begin to feel a sense of anticipation as you walk toward it. You feel, deep inside your soul, that this boulder has something very spiritual to share with you.

Reaching the boulder, you touch it, feeling the texture of the stone. You walk around the boulder to see if you can get a clearer view of what is hidden behind the boulder, and to see if there's a way you could climb it, to travel to the top of it. The rocks begin to metamorphose into a majestic stairway with twenty-two steps leading up into the universe, showing you a path.

You notice some of the steps open into a wide expanse of open meadows; other steps flow into plateaus, valleys, and gardens that stretch as far as the eye can see. Other steps form into open-arched doorways that invite you to travel within. Some steps appear to be moving, vibrating with energy as they shape into experiences that invite your soul to explore them.

You know this is a magical, mystical stairway to spirituality, and that each step you take on this stairway will give you important information about your spiritual nature and your soul, and everything it has experienced in all of its earthly and spiritual travels, in its eternal quest for truth and knowledge. You know there are steps your soul still needs to travel through the energies of to attain enlightenment.

Looking at all the steps on this stairway to spirituality, you see a word has been inscribed on each step. Your soul intuitively responds to and resonates with the words. You know that as you take each step, your soul will understand the true meaning and purpose inside each word, and how it relates to your evolvement. You know the words are really symbols of knowledge and as you explore the words and what they mean to you, they will open into experiences.

You look at the first step and see the word 'Existence.' You know this step leads you into the birth of your soul and shows you the path your soul has traveled in its ever-continuing journey of evolving. You look all the way to the top step and see the word 'Enlightenment.' You know that encompassed within and beyond this step are complete worlds of knowledge and experiences waiting for you to explore as you evolve ever higher.

Travel this stairway to spirituality that leads up into the universe, into the universal knowing within your soul. Explore each step on your soul's journey home to attain enlightenment.

# Metaphysical Master

――――――――――― ✑ ―――――――――――

*A metaphysical master gives you a yellow*
*rosebud that is just beginning to open up.*

In what appears to be a dream within a dream, a metaphysical master
speaks your name and gives you a small yellow rosebud that is just
beginning to open up. The stem is free from thorns, and the leaves
are green and healthy.

Holding the stem gently in your hand between your thumb and
forefinger, and turning the rosebud around slowly, looking at every
part of it, you admire its beauty, its perfect symmetry and balance.
Even though small, the rosebud is perfectly formed.

With your other hand, you touch it lovingly, caressing it, feeling
its velvety softness and its silky smoothness. Raising it to your nose,
you sniff its fragrant, pleasing aroma. Holding it gently, cradling the
bud in the palm of your hand, you realize this is a very special gift,
and you thank him for sharing it with you.

You know you need to care for the rosebud tenderly, to nurture
it with love and to nourish it with the energies of the universe. You
place it in a vase of water and put the vase in an open, sunny window.

There is a hope in your heart that the stem will root and you'll be
able to plant it, watching it grow into a beautiful rosebush and then
into a garden. Knowing this rosebud is very magical, you realize this
is possible.

The metaphysical master seems to know your thoughts. He smiles at you and asks you to meditate on the rosebud every day, watching it open up and unfold, petal by petal, as it reaches for the light of the sun. He asks you to do the same, to open up your mind and reach for the light of knowledge.

He asks you to notice how a dewdrop gently nourishes the bud in the early-morning hours, and how it gradually opens up and blooms into a very beautiful rose in the light of day and the warmth of the sun. He asks you to do the same, to nourish your mind with the energies of the universe, and to see your inner awareness expand and grow and bloom into a beautiful garden of spiritual knowledge.

Waking up from this dream with the scent of roses around you, you notice a few petals on your pillow.

Just a few thoughts for you to ponder: Maybe the yellow rosebud you imagined and created at the beginning of this book—when you were learning the language of your mind and starting to grow your imagination and open your inner knowing—is the same rosebud the metaphysical master has given you in this meditation.

And maybe this meditation, or perhaps all of life, is really just a dream, and you are your own teacher; you are the metaphysical master.

# Whirling White Light

*Be within a whirling beam of white light*
*to balance and blend your physical and*
*spiritual energies with universal energy.*

You are truly a powerful spiritual being of light. White light is very special and spiritual, and is yours simply for the asking. The following meditation will show you and share with you the universal energies you can tune into and touch with your mind and your spirit—for healing and many other positive purposes.

Imagine circles and spirals of white light that softly and gently vibrate around your physical body, moving slowly up and down in a flowing motion. Do this for a few moments to get into the flow of energy, to feel it around you, and to center your awareness within these whirling beams of white light.

You may begin to feel a pleasant sensation of warmth. You will also feel a special sense of freedom as you move and this white light moves with you, in perfect rhythm with your movements—in perfect synchronicity with your breathing as it begins to resonate with your own spiritual energies.

Draw these vibrations of powerful white light energies inside you so they are vibrating within you and through you as well as all around you. Breathe them inside you or simply absorb them within you, much as you experience the warmth of sunlight on your skin as it permeates your body.

Gradually, be and become one with the light. As you soak up the energies of the light within you, it balances and blends your physical and spiritual energies with universal energy to cleanse and purify your body, mind, and spirit, to heal you in every way, and to bring your physical consciousness into harmony with your spiritual awareness.

As the light permeates deep within you, it energizes and revitalizes you in every way as it clears all the cobwebs from your mind, cleanses the toxins from your body and your thoughts, frees your feelings and emotions from negativity, and opens up your full awareness of your true spiritual nature. It cleanses and purifies you on every level—body, mind, and spirit.

As you bring these whirling circles and spirals of white light inside you, and you are within the center of this energy vortex of universal vibrations, you experience a shower of awareness on a spiritual level—a sunburst of universal enlightenment.

As these circles and spirals of white light continue to encircle you and to vibrate within you, you realize how powerful they are—how powerful you are—and you simultaneously realize that this same energy resides in a reservoir deep inside you, welling up and releasing the spiritual power you have within you.

You sense and feel and know that the essence of your soul is intricately intertwined and interwoven with the universal vibrations of white light, and that your soul is completely in tune with and vibrates to the same energies as universal light.

You feel completely connected to the essence of this white light that permeates your entire being, healing and harmonizing every part of your body, mind, and spirit. As this gentle, loving energy flows through you, you know that this light, and all that it contains within itself, is your soul and that it is reawakening you to your true spiritual nature.

Explore and enjoy these whirling circles and spirals of white light energy. Experience the cleansing and healing of your body, mind, and spirit, and the complete opening up of your awareness.

When you're ready to end this meditation, gradually decrease the vibrations of energy, feeling and sensing the energies around you and within you slowing down to a physical level.

There is a knowingness deep inside you that white light is always instantly available to you and there are many practical and metaphysical applications for this energy; it works for any positive reason at any time.

This loving white light energy is your spiritual birthright to use in any way you desire. It always works for the highest good of all.

# Special Star

❧

*Travel the light of a very special star*
*to its source in the infinite universe.*

It's a beautiful, clear, moonlit evening. Gazing up at the millions of stars hanging gracefully in the universe in perfect symmetry, seeing their sparkling, radiant emanations of light as they shine brightly, you marvel that their light shines upon the earth, shines upon you. You wonder how this light is bright enough for you to see through the blackness, through the void of space.

Knowing that the light you see originated many thousands of years ago, perhaps eons ago, you begin to wonder about the origins of the stars. You wonder how they came into being, how they sustain themselves, why they were created, and for what purpose.

You begin to wonder about your source, your origin, how you came into being, how your soul began life, and what initiated your creation. You wonder if your soul was born the same way the stars were born, and how long your soul has existed.

One star catches your attention as it twinkles brightly in the sky, shining its light upon you. You feel an affinity with this star. It seems to be a very special star, calling to you and inviting you into its light, asking you to travel the light of this star to its source. You sense yourself traveling through the sky, through the infinite universe on the energy of light from the star, going back in time as the light draws you to its source.

Thoughts and images begin to race through your mind; you wonder if you are also being drawn toward the source of what you think might be your beginning of life, might be the beginning of you—the birth of your soul.

Zooming on the vibration of light, you are going faster and faster, traveling at the speed of light and even faster through space, seeing, knowing, remembering every experience you've ever had in every moment of life, as a physical being and as a spiritual being, in every form your soul has ever been in. You remember every multidimensional aspect of your soul, in all of its many vibrations and expressions.

Looking at all the stars and the planets that surround you, you remember living on some of them. Your memories are very clear and vivid. Flashes of recognition zip in and out of your awareness quickly, yet you have full comprehension and complete understanding of every experience, every event and emotion, every second of every life, and you see with a clarity that goes way beyond human comprehension.

You're so very far above the earth now. Looking down at the earth—the beautiful green and blue globe that you call home for the present moment—you remember and re-experience every moment of every life you've had on earth.

Continuing to hurtle through the universe, through space, you realize it isn't a black void as you first thought. It is filled with a life and vibrancy and energy that is continuous and ever-changing.

At last, you reach the star that beckoned to you, the special star that invited you to travel its light, to see and experience its source. This star shares the knowledge of its birth and its source of light with you. Walking around this star, seeing and knowing its origin and life-force, its energy vibration, you begin to wonder again about the birth of your soul.

Was the birth of your soul similar to the birth of this star? Or maybe your soul was born on this star, and that's why you could travel its light source so easily. Or did seeing the origin and birth of this star simply remind you of the birth of your soul?

As you watch the beginnings—the birth of this star—memories of your origin begin to come into your mind. Vague at first, then becoming clearer and more focused as you center your awareness and attention on them, and you see and remember the beginnings and birth of your soul, the beginning of your light in the universe.

Knowing and experiencing the birth of this star, you recognize that its beginnings are similar to your soul's beginnings. With your remembrance, you travel to a special place in the universe to reunite and reconnect with your spiritual source.

It's a dimension of being-ness where your soul was born and where you return, time and time again, to your source to renew yourself—your spiritual essence and awareness, your light—after every lifetime, after every existence, wherever you have lived before.

You experience a sense of timelessness as your soul's multidimensional awareness opens up completely. It's as if the star you explored exists just as much in the future as in the past, and its light is never-ending and always-becoming. You know, too, that your soul is timeless, that it has always existed and will always exist.

As you remember your birth—your soul's beginnings, the creation of your spiritual essence when your awareness was born—you realize there is no death, no end, that your soul is continuous and exists forever, that your light shines brightly, both in this world and in other worlds, and the light of your soul goes on forever.

You gaze up at the special star in the universe that shared its source with you and invited you within its light. Seeing its sparkling, radiant emanations of light as it shines brightly in the universe, you marvel at the light of the star and at the light of your soul as it shines brightly, sharing its light with the earth.

# Bridge of Light

*Discover and travel a bridge of light between the earth and the universe, between the physical and the spiritual worlds, as you blend your inner and outer worlds together.*

You are so much more than a physical being. You are a powerful, radiant, spiritual being of light. You can journey beyond time and space into the non-physical realm your soul lives in when you're not here on earth to see what your soul experiences in its pure energy form of light.

You'll travel a bridge of light between the earth and the universe, between the physical and the spiritual, as you journey into the pure energy of your spirit, as you travel between both worlds to see what your soul sees and to know what your soul knows. This meditation can show you how to bring your spiritual awareness into every aspect of your life.

---

You see a bridge in the distance that is shimmering and sparkling with ethereal energy, yet the luminous bridge appears to have physical substance and form. You know somehow that it bridges both worlds—the earth and the universe, the physical and the spiritual—blending them and bringing them together.

You've heard there are bridges of light called rainbow bridges which span both worlds, that rainbow bridges are magical and mystical, and they offer gifts and treasures to anyone who can see the bridge and travel it.

You've never seen a rainbow bridge before and you feel excited about this discovery. You've walked this way many times before, looking at the same spot in the distance, but this is the first time you've seen the bridge. You wonder if it has always been there and you just weren't able to see it, or if it has somehow magically appeared today just for you.

You notice that the worlds are side-by-side, not above and below as you may have always believed. This seems a bit strange to you at first, then you realize it's perfectly natural and wonder why you never perceived it this way before.

Both worlds vibrate together, a mere frequency or vibration or perception apart, yet both worlds are simultaneous, each one intimately and intricately influencing and affecting the other.

As you walk toward the bridge, you notice the vibrations of light that form the bridge are interwoven and in continuous motion. The sparkles and shimmers interplay with each other, creating a gentle movement, as if a soft breeze is flowing through the energy vibrations.

You feel a sense of exhilaration as you wonder what it would be like to walk upon this bridge. You notice the bridge is perfectly formed; it rises up gently in an arch in the center, just as a rainbow arches across the heavens. You see the handrails on both sides that have been formed with tendrils of luminous light.

You're not able to see where the bridge ends; it stretches into the universe, into infinity, far beyond what your eye can see. You begin to wonder what is on the other side of the bridge and think there must be something very spiritual on the other side. You decide you'd like to see what's there, what's beyond your physical line of vision.

You walk forward more quickly, eager to reach the bridge and begin to travel it. You have a magical sense of what awaits you. A feeling of wonderful anticipation builds inside you with every step.

You've now reached the bridge. Putting your hand on one of the handrails, you feel a gentle flow of energy from the bridge in your fingertips. It's an effervescent bubbling sensation; it feels pleasant and somehow the feeling is very familiar to you.

Stepping on this rainbow bridge of light between the earth and the universe that spans and bridges together the physical and spiritual worlds, you notice it's sturdy, secure, and safe. Even though it sways a bit, you know it's the motion of energy that makes it vibrate and move.

You feel the gentle vibration of energy from the bridge begin to radiate upward through you, beginning with your feet. It's the same gentle sensation you felt in your fingertips. You know this is a magical, mystical bridge and that it can take you above and across the earth into the universe, above and beyond your physical self into your soul.

You wonder what you'll find as you cross this bridge. Moving forward to explore what is in front of you, the gentle vibration of energy reassures you and invites to travel this bridge, this rainbow between the worlds.

Travel the bridge of light to see where it takes you and what it shows you. Walk across this bridge to see what you'll find on this bridge and on the other side of the bridge.

Along the way, perhaps you will see an angel who meets you halfway and offers to guide you into and through the realms beyond the bridge. Or perhaps you will choose to travel by yourself, guided by your inner knowing, as you bridge the physical and spiritual worlds, and bring them together within yourself.

# Rainbow Path

---◆ ❧ ◆---

*Travel a more-than-magical journey through a
shimmering rainbow in the sky to find spiritual
gifts within the vibrations of each color.*

Your spiritual self has many treasures to offer you; gifts that are just
waiting for you to see them and accept them. Let yourself completely
experience the gift that is offered. These gifts are presented to you
from your soul and are given to you for you to use in any way you
desire to make your life better in every way, and to reflect the essence
of your soul.

---◆ ❧ ◆---

Imagine an early morning rainfall. Listen to the sound of the rain
as it gently taps on the glass of the window in your bedroom. The
sound is lulling and soothing, comforting and relaxing.

You feel as if you're dreaming; you're inside a magical, wonderful dream. As the soft, steady rhythm of the rain continues, you feel
peaceful and quiet within yourself. Rising from your bed, you look
out the window, noticing it's nearly dawn and the sun is just beginning to rise, emerging from behind white, misty clouds, spreading its
light over the earth.

You think this is a bit curious—that the sun can be seen through
the clouds. Then you look up at the sky and see the most beautiful

rainbow you've ever seen. It's shimmering in the light reflected from the sun, radiating sparkles of rainbow-colored light everywhere.

You feel the rainbow shimmering all around you as you gaze up at it. It's magical and mystical, with a special aura all around it, and you begin to get a sense of the vibrant energies flowing through the rainbow. You wonder what it would be like to fly up into and through this magical, mystical rainbow to experience the awe and wonder and joy of it with every part of your being.

There is a knowing inside you that by traveling inside this rainbow, and totally immersing yourself within all the many soft and subtle hues and vibrations of the colors, and involving all your senses in exploring and experiencing the rainbow with every part of your awareness—seeing, touching, tasting, smelling, and hearing the harmony and joy of it—you could become the essence of the shimmering, sparkling rainbow, experiencing the awe and wonder and joy of it with every part of your being.

You'd feel the energies of the colors vibrating all around you, through you, and within every part of you—pulsating inside your heart, flowing within your body, embracing your mind, encircling your soul.

You want to feel the vibrations of the rainbow sparkling and shimmering and emanating from within your body—from within the center of your being, the very core of your soul—and radiating outward from you. You want to become a rainbow of colors, vibrating and shimmering in a magical flow and radiance of energy, expanding both inward and outward.

You listen as the raindrops begin to patter slowly now as the rain softly comes to an end. As you step outside, everything looks bright and beautiful. Breathe in the freshness of the gentle breeze and experience the wonderful, refreshing feeling of a rain shower that has just ended.

Looking up at the sky, you see the beautiful rainbow shimmering and sparkling in the sunlight. The colors of the rainbow are vibrant and pure, a shimmering spectrum of colors blending into one another, vibrating perfectly in tune with each other, creating harmony within your mind and soul. It's the most beautiful rainbow you've ever seen. It surrounds you like a perfect dome that touches the earth and the sky.

A magical, wonderful, joyful feeling enters your body, your heart, your mind, and your soul. You feel as if you could reach up and touch the rainbow. You feel as if you could breathe in the colors and be inside them. You feel as if you could rise through the rainbow from beginning to end, and discover a treasure at the end of the rainbow.

As you're admiring the beauty of the rainbow and sensing the harmony of the colors, you decide you're going to take a magical journey through the rainbow to experience and absorb the colors within your body, your mind, and your soul. More than anything else at the moment, you want to feel what the colors are really like. You want to be inside the colors and in tune with the colors, to feel their rhythm and harmony.

You want to become the rainbow, you want to feel the light vibrating in harmony with your soul, in tune with your spiritual essence. You want to experience and understand the energies and vibrations of each color. You want to see what's inside each color; you want to be each color. With those thoughts, the shimmering, sparkling rainbow in the universe invites you to travel its colors. Somehow you know that all you have to do is just relax into the rainbow and feel yourself flowing upward through the colors.

You feel yourself rising up into the rainbow, floating upward, rising into the color red at the bottom of the rainbow. You feel the color all around you. Breathing in the color, you feel it inside you, gently moving through your body. Absorbing the color within your mind, you feel your mind opening up and becoming more aware.

Within the color red, you see a majestic mountain before you, filled with trees and grassy meadows, gardens and rivers, hills and valleys, plateaus and waterfalls that are touched and highlighted with rainbow colors. You know you're grounded in the earth, in your physical awareness. You sense the energy of this mountain, the energy of you. Explore the mountain's energy that is in harmony with your energy inside the color red to see what it has to offer you and to find a wonderful gift from your soul.

Feeling drawn to the vibrations of the color orange, you feel yourself rising up into the color within the rainbow. Breathing in the color, you become part of the color and the color becomes part of you. You feel it inside you and all around you.

Absorbing the color within your mind, you experience a wonderful feeling of freedom. You feel as if you're standing on the earth and in the sky at the same time. Within the color orange, you see an opening—an arched doorway—that has been formed between two boulders in the mountainside.

It seems to be lit from within; the glowing orange light beckons you to explore and see what is in there. As you enter into the rich deepness of your mind, you become aware of a special gift within this opening, a spiritual gift that will help you in any way you choose in your life right now.

As you exit the open doorway, you feel yourself expanding into the rainbow, into the color yellow, the color of sunshine. Breathing in the color, you feel its light moving gently within and through your body, within and through your mind. As your mind opens up and becomes more aware, you understand the quality and nature of the rainbow, and you understand the quality and nature of inner truth and knowledge. You feel your inner awareness expanding and increasing.

Within the color yellow, you notice the bright sunshine all around you. It feels warm on your skin and you allow the warmth to fill your body, your mind, and your spirit. Absorbing the sunlight within you, you feel it permeating every part of you with a pleasant, gentle warmth and you feel your mind opening up in the light.

Looking up at the sun, you notice the shafts of light are like a god's eye, filtering through a cloud from the heavens. One ray of light is especially bright, and is much larger and wider than the others. It calls to you gently and you decide to see what makes it sparkle.

As you walk forward into the light, you feel it resonating within you, permeating your soul. You see a podium before you, a lectern where perhaps a wise professor or philosopher would give lectures to students. On the podium, you see a book of knowledge that is open and waiting for you. Walk over to it and read the book to see what knowledge and spiritual gifts it has to offer you.

Cradling your book of knowledge in your arms, close to your heart, knowing it contains the truth about your soul, you travel into the color green. Breathing it inside you, you feel its vibrations resonating in harmony within and through your body. As you experience it vibrating within your mind and your heart, you become in touch with your inner feelings. You feel the color with your emotions; you feel the color nourishing your body as well as your mind. Within the color green, you see a lush, beautiful garden, a perfect place of peaceful healing, a spiritual sanctuary.

You decide to visit this garden, perhaps to read more of the book or to just relax and enjoy the peaceful beauty and serenity of nature, to feel the tranquility nurture your soul, and to fully appreciate the flowers that are budding and blooming there. Your heart feels complete joy at being in this beautiful healing place of harmony.

As you breathe in the pure, fresh, clean air, and the scent of the greenness and the pleasing fragrance of the flowers all around you, you feel the air and the greenness and the wonderful, fragrant aroma of the flowers in this garden revitalizing and rejuvenating you, filling every part of your body, mind, and spirit with perfect health and harmony.

You feel refreshed and healthy as you look up at the beautiful blue sky above you and notice the expansiveness of the universe. The blue seems to go on forever. Rising up into the color blue, floating and rising higher inside the rainbow, you feel peaceful and tranquil.

Breathing in the color, you feel as if your thoughts are words, and your words are images that spring into action through your feelings. You feel as if you can say and see your thoughts at the same time, that they're really one and the same, with no difference between the thought and the word. You have a wonderful knowing and understanding that the sky and the earth are really one and the same, with no difference between the universe and you.

You feel as if you're in tune with the universe, and you know that as you ascend into the blue, you can communicate with the sky and, in turn, the sky will share its secrets with you. Converse with the sky; listen to what it says to you, hear what it tells you, see what it shows you, and accept what it offers you.

As you're traveling through the sky, learning its wisdom, remembering your soul's wisdom, you rise up into the color indigo inside the rainbow. Breathing the color of intuitive awareness and inner knowing inside you, your mind completely opens up and expands into ever-widening horizons that go far beyond what can be physically seen and touched. You have an understanding and a knowing that goes beyond words and feelings.

You see a purplish-blue cloud, an indigo cloud, that your soul feels a familiarity with. It reminds you of the strength of the thundercloud that brought the early morning rainfall. As you remember the gentleness of the rain, a peaceful feeling comes over you, an intuitive knowingness of the power within the cloud, the power within you.

As you enter the cloud, you see an indigo flower in its center, and you know the past, present, and future of this flower. You see it first as a bud, just beginning to open up, and you realize it is your spiritual awareness, beginning to open up.

Watch as the indigo flower continues to open up, as your awareness continues to open up, to bloom and blossom into inner wisdom and knowledge, into the realness of inner knowing and spiritual awareness, into the essence of your soul.

As you're meditating on this flower, watching it open up, seeing your inner knowing open up, you ascend into the color violet at the top of the rainbow above the indigo cloud. Breathing the color violet inside you, feeling it circulate within you, the color inspires feelings of awe and reverence, wonder and joy. You realize you've opened up your mind's awareness, and are experiencing your true spiritual nature. You've opened up the knowing inside your soul, and you understand all that is within you.

Within the color violet, you feel special, sacred. You close your eyes for a moment, to fully absorb the color within yourself, breathing it in, feeling it permeating every part of you. When you open your eyes, you see a beautiful chapel on the top of the mountain that was temporarily hidden from view until you raised your awareness into the sky and the universe.

Enter the chapel and see what is within. Your gift is within. Perhaps it is a tangible gift. Perhaps it is a prayer that has been answered, a desire that has been granted, or perhaps it is a sense of direction that you know you must follow to travel the rainbow path inside your soul.

As you leave the chapel at the top of this mountain—at the top of the rainbow—you peer down through the misty clouds at the earth below, seeing through the illusions that may have previously clouded your spiritual vision of your physical experiences. Breathing in the light of the early-morning rays of sunshine and the pure, clean air, you feel them flowing through you, refreshing and rejuvenating your spirit.

You feel as if you are waking up from a wonderful dream, and you know you're waking up to your spiritual self. You feel a pull from your physical self and know it's time to come back down to earth from your rainbow travels.

As you re-enter the rainbow, you feel yourself gradually descending through all the colors you've experienced. You feel yourself softly blending into the colors of violet, indigo, blue, green, yellow, orange, and red, remembering all the wonderful things you experienced and the spiritual gifts you've received in each color.

Now you're standing on the ground again, looking up at the rainbow above you. You notice the sunshine, as it begins to disperse all the clouds. The rainbow seemingly disappears into the light, yet you know it is still there, ready to appear when you are ready to see it again. Reflecting on your rainbow journey, you know you've discovered a special treasure within yourself, within your soul.

# Light Library

⌒

*Visit a library of light and read a very*
*special book that's all about your soul.*
*Watch as the words come to life*
*and portray your experiences.*

You see a spiral stairway composed of rays of light shimmering into the universe. Placing your foot on the bottom step, you feel a gentle wave of energy flow through you. As you travel up the stairs, the vibration of energy softly radiates upward from your feet through your entire body. You feel as if you're floating a few inches above the steps, gliding through emanations of energy, weightless and free, flowing into higher realms of light.

The top of the stairs are shrouded in a soft, white mist. As you enter the mist, it clears, showing a vibrant path shimmering with light. Following the path, you feel the pure white light envelop you with a very pleasant warmth. Breathing in the energy of light, it fills you with a wonderful feeling of peace and harmony.

A few steps ahead, the light illuminates a shimmering building in an open, circular area. The building radiates a special kind of energy that resonates with your soul. Stepping into the light, you enter a library that is created entirely with the vibrant energy of the light.

Windows reflect rays of universal light everywhere. Vibrations of light form the floors and the walls. Beams of sparkling energy support the arched ceiling; in the center is a domed skylight. A magical aura surrounds the library; ethereal energies of pure awareness softly reverberate through the vast array of books.

A hushed stillness echoes within the library even as it shimmers with energy, with the knowledge contained in the books that fill the shelves and line the walls. As you listen quietly, you hear the books talk in whispers of wisdom and murmurs of mystical knowledge.

The rows of books appear to be endless, as if they go on forever. Walking through the aisles and the alcoves, you see books on every subject imaginable. This library contains all the knowledge that has ever been written or recorded in all the world and the entire universe since the beginning of time, since the beginning of thought.

Running your fingers over the titles of the books, you feel a shimmer of energy go through you and discover you can read them within your mind. The books are written in a universal language you understand easily, just by touching the books or looking at the pictures on the covers. The words and their images dance into your mind, creating a symphony of sound vibrations; within the music and the melody, you understand the knowledge inside each book.

Continuing to walk through the library, exploring the light energies of knowledge, you notice another stairway with seven steps that vibrate with a light more dazzling, more brilliant than the light that surrounded the open entrance to the library. The light shimmers and sparkles with energy as if it's alive.

There's a sacred feeling about this light; it seems to contain an essence within itself. The vibrations emanating from this light are filled with images of color that have shape and substance. It looks like a beautiful blur of rainbow colors in a gentle wave of motion, forming into ever-changing transparent prisms of light. Looking into the light, you experience an emotion that goes beyond words and thoughts, and you know you're about to enter a very sacred space.

More than anything else, you want to be part of that light. You want to rush into the light, to become the essence of the light, yet feel you might disturb it if you rush, so you wait respectfully and reverently. The light opens up and invites you in, just as the light at the entrance to the library welcomed you in. Stepping into the light, you're filled with a feeling of awe and wonderment and pure joy.

Each step of the stairway vibrates in harmony with the colors of a rainbow. Walking slowly, thoughtfully, up the stairs, you pause on every step—feeling the energy, hearing the unique vibration, the tone and hue and experience of each color. Ascending the stairs and absorbing the colors within you, you become more and more aware of your soul. As your awareness expands, you know you're traveling a stairway that leads you into the true essence of yourself.

Reaching the top of the stairs, you see that the higher echelon of the library is a loft that contains the written records of every soul's existence, and you know, with a magical sense of inner knowing, that these books vibrate with a light that is unique to every soul and can only be opened and read by that particular soul.

In the center of the loft, you see a table with an open book and a lamp that glows with a luminous light. Next to the table is a comfortable chair. You walk over to the table and look at the book. It seems the library has been waiting for you to discover it, and the open book has been waiting to be read by you.

Knowing the book is about your soul, you look at the chapter title the book is opened to. As you read the words, they begin to vibrate on the page, then to shimmer with a soft glow of light, emanating into rays of energy that form images that swirl into your thoughts and sparkle into pictures, opening a special kind of knowing within your mind.

Touching the words, your hand begins to vibrate with energy. You realize how very special this book is. Picking it up, you settle comfortably in the chair. Holding the open book in your hands, your body begins to vibrate with a radiant energy. You feel as if you're being drawn inside the pages of the book as the words vibrate and resonate in your mind, moving in rhythm and harmony with the flow of spiritual and universal energy.

It feels as if a gentle current of energy is flowing through you. You hear a soft humming sound inside your mind, and as the energy continues to softly flow through you, you know your spiritual awareness is completely opening up inside you. Hugging the book close to your heart, you know you've found a very special treasure—a book that reveals all your spiritual knowledge, a book that shows you the secrets of your soul.

You read the chapter title again; the words form an image that draws a complete and detailed picture in your mind. You touch the picture in the book, the picture in your mind, feeling the texture of the images. The pictures are solid. The scene is real; it isn't an image that disappears when you blink your eyes.

*The words form real pictures.* When you read the words, they form pictures that come to life—three-dimensional images that vibrate from the pages into your awareness, into your physical reality—resonating with an energy source that is inspired by the words on the pages.

The book is energy in motion and the words magically transport you into the scene. You're there, inside the picture; you're really there. Looking all around, you see and feel and experience everything there is to see and feel and experience. The book is filled with every experience you've ever had or will have, and yet you know you can write and rewrite the pages and paragraphs in any way you choose.

As you look through the pages and read the words that have already been written, your experiences come to life, and you completely understand—with a clarity and knowing that goes beyond words—why they happened and why you chose to experience them. You feel—with every part of you, with every part of your awareness—the events and emotions inside your experiences as the words draw detailed and descriptive images and scenes within your mind.

The book is timeless as it portrays the pictures of your soul—the essence of your spirit—as it speaks to you of the events and emotions in your life, and shows you the many, various aspects of all your experiences in every time frame—past, present, and future—and in every dimension of being, in every realm of your awareness. The book shows you the true reality of you—the true multidimensionality of your soul.

# Realms of Reality

_____ ᦞ _____

*From somewhere in another reality, an*
*image, or a dream, or a memory appears.*

This is a completely self-guided meditation, a very special inner journey. Allow an image or a dream or a memory to form in your mind. Accept and acknowledge whatever appears in the way that it shows itself. Let it come into full focus and form.

Explore and experience every aspect of it. Know that it is real and true and valid. Guided by your inner knowing, let your mind show you the many wonders inside you; let your mind share with you the secrets of your soul and the true realities of your multidimensional self.

As the image, dream, or memory—or perhaps what you perceive as an entirely new experience—appears in your mind, you may experience an intense feeling of déjà vu—of having been there before or of having experienced the scene before, but without quite remembering where or when.

You have an absolute knowing that it really happened, but you're not sure if it occurred in a physical place, or somewhere inside your mind, or perhaps in another realm of your reality.

Clearly pinpoint the image, thought, feeling, scene, event, experience, or place by completely focusing on and sensing the vibrations and energies associated with it. Keep in mind that time and space are fluid in this deeper realm of reality, this inner dimension of your mind.

Immerse yourself totally in your meditation. Go with the flow of your thoughts and feelings. Center in on what your mind shares with you and shows you. See everything there is to see, and know everything there is to know.

# Revolving Earth

——————— ❧ ———————

*Journey through the infinite reach of time and space*
*to experience and explore into you've lived before, and to*
*see your soul in an expansive, luminous vibration of light.*

Imagine you're on a sandy beach on a pleasantly warm, beautiful summer day, watching the waves as they come to the shore and return to the ocean, listening to the ebb and flow of the tide.

This place, this day, this moment is absolutely perfect and you feel a wonderful sense of contentment and peace being here. The sun is warm and pleasant on your body, and you feel a gentle breeze caress you softly.

See and feel yourself in this safe, soothing, peaceful place on the beach on the most beautiful day you've ever experienced. You feel so relaxed and comfortable here. You're in tune with the harmony of the waves and in harmony with yourself. The sound of the water is peaceful and soothing, relaxing you more and more.

You decide to lie down on the soft sand of this beautiful beach, resting on the warm sand as you listen to the motion of the waves and watch the blueness of the sky above you.

You notice a few puffy white clouds in the sky that are just floating along. You feel so in tune with them; you're just floating along in a comfortable rhythm and motion of harmony.

Your spirit feels free and light, as free as the clouds that float above you. As you're breathing in and out, you continue to watch the clouds in the sky as they float by. Take another deep breath in, feeling it fill you completely. As you let it out very slowly, you know your breath is like the ocean with waves of time coming and going, matching the rhythm of your breath as you inhale and exhale.

As the waves ebb and flow, you breathe in and out. Listen to the waves as they come up to the shore and as they recede into the ocean. Listen to your breathing as you breathe in and out, slowly and naturally.

Listen to the sound of the waves as you breathe in and out, as the waves of time ebb and flow. You're breathing in and out, in a natural rhythm and flow that is in harmony with the tides, breathing in harmony with the ebb and flow of time.

As you breathe in, you feel your spiritual essence expanding with your breath, becoming lighter than air. You feel very free and open, expansive and light. As you breathe out, you feel the essence of your spirit leaving your body, rising up into the air, floating freely and easily away from your physical body, traveling on your breath, floating through the air, just like the clouds floating leisurely along in the beautiful blue sky above you.

You feel weightless and free. You feel so weightless and free that your awareness—your spirit—begins to float upward toward the clouds in the sky. It's a safe, comfortable, natural feeling, as natural as breathing and listening to the sound of the waves.

Feel your awareness—your spiritual essence—continue to float upward, slowly, bit by bit. Your spirit seems to expand and rise on your breath as you breathe in and out. Your breath cushions you like a gentle current of air as you rise higher and higher. Breathe in, becoming lighter than air. Breathe out, floating on a soft current of air.

As you're floating through the sky, you become aware of a soft radiant white light that is filtering through your mind as you enter one of the beautiful white clouds in the sky. As you breathe in the light, you're aware of your soul, flowing into a timeless realm.

You feel your mind—your soul—flowing into a vast, infinite sea of white light, an essence so ethereal and luminous that words cannot describe it. See and feel this gentle, illuminating energy as it bathes your mind with the higher wisdom and eternal essence of your soul. Breathe this light inside you; feel it circulating in and through your body, your mind, and your soul.

As you feel the energies of white light softly entering your mind and gently circulating through your body, you become completely aware of your soul and you know that you are an eternal, spiritual being. You know that your soul is timeless. You're aware of the freedom you have to go beyond the limits of your physical consciousness, beyond the restrictions of physical time and space.

You know you can go anywhere in time and space, into any past experience simply by placing your awareness and attention there. You know time and space are illusions of physical reality. In the multidimensional energy of your soul, time and space do not exist. You know your soul is part of that infinite essence of light that is beyond time and space.

Breathe in and be in the light. Be and become one with the light. Be and become one with your soul. Be the light; be your soul. Breathe out the light and feel it expanding all around you. Breathe in the light and feel it expanding within you.

Within the ethereal essence of white light, you see a guide who is waiting to journey with you as you travel into and through the vibrations of time. You experience a wonderful feeling of complete trust and feel a positive attunement with your soul guide.

Your guide is part of your soul and knows everything there is to know about all your experiences in your past lives. Your inner guide will show you events and emotions in your past lives and will explain how they interconnect with and weave through the experiences in your present life to give you a complete understanding of those experiences.

Your guide says it is time to begin your journey, and asks if you are ready to explore the experiences and emotions in your past lives.

As you answer yes, you move toward your guide to reconnect with the essence of your soul.

Your guide reaches out to you. As you embrace, you merge your physical and spiritual energies together. As you take the hand of your guide, you feel yourself floating through time, floating through a vast infinite sea of time.

Your awareness is floating, flowing through the ethereal essence of light as you travel into and through the infinite reaches of time— going into time, through time, beyond time, above time.

Your awareness is in a place of luminous light, a light that is vibrating with energy, with the essence of life. Your awareness is flowing and floating gently through this light, through the vibrations of time as you begin your journey with your soul guide, who will show you the experiences in your past lives and how they interconnect with the experiences in your present life.

Breathing in and out, feeling expansive—lighter than air and floating on a gentle current of air—you feel the essence of your spirit rising up even higher into the air, above the clouds. Your spirit is expansive and light, and can travel anywhere you wish.

You flow through the vibrations of time with your guide—seeing, knowing, and understanding all the things you see and experience. Breathing in harmony with your spirit, your awareness travels on the gentle rhythm and energy of your breath. You feel yourself soaring, gliding, rising even higher in the air.

Floating freely in the air, you observe the world below you. Your guide asks you to look at the earth—the home where your soul resides now. You see a great expanse of ocean below you.

As you watch the waves ebb and flow, you feel the rhythm of the tides, the rhythm of time, as you breathe in and out. You see the various shades of blue in the ocean and the ripple of the waves.

You feel the gentle current of air as you float above the vibrations of time, above the energies of the earth. You rise up even higher into the air far above the earth, looking at the beautiful blue and green earth below you, revolving slowly in the universe. You see the majesty of the heavens and the panorama of the universe.

A feeling of timelessness surrounds you; you know that time, as you normally perceive it, does not exist for your soul. You know you can travel into the past just as easily as you are in the present. You notice your vision and awareness are also expanded.

You see places in the earth that have a special connection for you in the past, places where you've lived before. These places call to your spirit, beckoning you to visit.

As the earth revolves below you, you feel your spirit being drawn to a place on earth where you've lived before, a place that has a special reason and purpose for you to explore now, a place that will provide you with meaningful information you can bring back with you into your present life. Your spirit floats easily and softly on a gentle current of air into the place where you've lived before.

As your spirit begins to explore this physical place on earth, you notice you have an expanded view and an increased understanding of all the things that occurred here in your past life and why they happened. You see souls you know now who were with you in that past life.

Your spirit shows you all the experiences you had in your past life that have created the present you're now experiencing. You see how the present and the past are interwoven through the threads of time.

Completely explore the experiences you've become aware of to see what happened in the past life and to understand why it happened. Listen to your soul guide as your inner knowing—your spiritual awareness—speaks to you through your thoughts and feelings as you observe and participate in the events and emotions that were part of your past life here, and to see how your past life experiences affect your present life.

When you're done exploring everything you want to know about this past life, your spirit rises into the air above the earth with your soul guide. You again notice how the green and blue earth revolves below you.

If you wish, you may visit another location where you've lived before that has a special meaning and purpose for you now. You may visit as many places as your soul desires for you to see and experience. Explore the experiences you've had there to understand why they occurred and how they're connected with your present life.

When you're done with your past life travels, you feel your spirit rising into the universe above the earth as your soul guide accompanies you. You feel your essence return to the ethereal, luminous white light, and you're aware of being in this infinite sea of white light.

Your guide takes you into the multidimensional energies of your soul to show you where you live when your soul is not experiencing a life on earth.

Explore this land of spirit; re-experience what your soul knows. See what your soul shows you. Listen to what your soul says to you. Be there for a while in the light, in this land of spirit, in the home of your soul, to reflect on everything you became aware of during your past life journey.

Talk to your guide; ask any questions you have so you can reach a higher understanding of all the things you experienced on your trip through time.

When you are done with your reflections and you're ready to return to what your physical self perceives as your present reality in this lifetime, bid your soul guide good-bye. Thank this wonderful guide who showed you the experiences your soul has had, who gave you insights into your soul and provided you with answers as you saw the events and emotions in your past lives, and in the multidimensional realm of your spirit.

Your guide embraces you and gives you a special gift to bring back with you into your physical reality. Watch your guide go into the pure essence of white light, knowing you may call upon your guide at any time you want or need to, and for any reason.

When you're ready to come back down to earth, you feel your spirit flowing through the universe as you turn your attention toward earth. You again see the great expanse of ocean below you, moving in a natural rhythm and harmony with both the earth and the universe.

You slowly and gently float down into a beautiful white cloud in the sky. Your spirit travels on your breath, returning to your physical body, returning you to the place here on earth that you call home now, to the place where you are right now.

Gliding gently back down to earth, you land softly on the sand of the beach where you began your journey through time. You see the ocean and hear the waves as they move in rhythm and harmony, as the waves of time ebb and flow. You feel the breath of your spiritual essence as you breathe in and out.

You hear the rhythm and harmony of your soul, in tune with the natural flow of the earth and the universe. Breathing in and out, you bring with you the full awareness and understanding of your soul and all that it has experienced in your travels through time.

# Elevator to Awareness

         ∽

*A magical elevator transports you through time and space
into the awareness of all the experiences of your soul.*

You're in a beautiful, serene place in nature—a meadow filled with early-morning light. Looking around, you see thousands of vibrant, colorful flowers in bloom. The sun is rising and feels pleasantly warm. The light is bright, welcoming you on an inner journey.

Looking around this peaceful meadow, you notice the sunlight sparkling on what appears to be an elevator with glass sides so you may see all around you when you journey. You know this elevator to awareness will take you anywhere you wish to travel through time, to see and know all the experiences of your soul. The elevator doors open, waiting for you to enter.

As you enter the elevator, you intuitively know where your soul wants to go and what you need to experience right now. This elevator has no numbers for floors; instead, the buttons have lights with beautiful hues of colors. When you touch a button, you hear a soft, musical sound and you feel the energy that emanates from that particular button.

These magical, musical buttons allow you to travel through time. The sound of each button when you reach toward it inspires a knowing within your soul and opens an inner awareness about what sort of experiences you'll discover if you push that certain button.

You look at all the buttons, but before you can touch one of them, the elevator begins to move gently, gliding through time. The feeling of traveling in this elevator is calming and soothing, and you feel a distinct sensation of movement, a journeying of your awareness traveling through time, floating through the spaces of time, flowing into the experiences of your soul.

You begin to feel a wonderful sense of anticipation inside you, knowing, somehow, that you are about to have a very special experience. The elevator doors open into a beautiful garden that is green and lush, filled with a multitude of flowers that are colorful and vibrant, swaying softly in the gentle breeze. You smell the wonderful, sweet fragrance of the flowers as the pleasing scent wafts to you through the air.

The harmony of the scene beckons you, calling you to visit. You feel your soul being drawn into the garden. You feel complete peace and harmony within yourself in this beautiful, spiritual place, and you know you're perfectly in tune with your soul.

In the center of the garden, you see a shimmering light and sense a special, loving presence is waiting for you. As you enter the garden, you see a spiritual guide who will accompany you on your journey.

Perhaps you've already met your guide in one of your dreams, or your guide has appeared at other times in your life to help you in a special way, or maybe you recognize your guide as your higher self.

Your guide comes forward to greet you, embracing you lovingly. You feel yourself blending into the spiritual essence of your guide, and you feel completely comfortable and utterly happy to be with your guide.

Your guide asks if you are ready to begin your journey and walks with you back to the elevator. As you enter the elevator through the open doors, you notice one of the buttons sparkles with energy; it seems to call to you.

You reach out to touch the button. Almost before your hand touches it, you hear the soft musical sound as the elevator moves effortlessly through time. You feel your spirit gently and easily flowing into and through a timeless realm of awareness in tune with the musical sound you hear.

The elevator begins to slow and then stop; the doors open into a soul experience that is important for you to become aware of now. As you exit the elevator, see where you are and what is around you. Notice what your thoughts and feelings are, and what is happening. Your guide can help you understand the significance of this soul experience, and why you've journeyed here.

When you've completely explored this experience your soul has shown you, you return to the elevator, knowing there is another soul experience for you to explore. As you touch one of the buttons, you hear the soft musical sound and feel your soul moving into another experience.

Again, be fully in the experience. See and explore everything that is important for you to know about this experience. On this journey through your soul, you may visit as many experiences as you desire.

When you are done with your soul journeys, you return to the magical elevator. You hear the soft, musical sound again as the elevator moves through time. The elevator doors open with a soft, whooshing sound into the peaceful meadow where you began your journey.

If you'd like, spend some time there to reflect on everything you've become aware of. Talk with your soul—your guide—to ask any questions you may have or to reach a higher understanding of everything you've experienced on your soul journey.

Your guide embraces you and bids you goodbye, giving you a gift. As you open it, you realize the gift is the awareness that your guide is always with you, helping you, protecting you, loving you, and bringing you the awareness of your soul in all your experiences.

When you are ready to return to your present reality, you enter the elevator again, the elevator that transported you so easily and effortlessly into the awareness of your soul. Standing in the elevator, you look at all the multicolored buttons with their magical, musical sounds that allow you to travel through time, and you know you can journey into your soul again whenever you wish in this elevator to awareness.

Pushing the button that brings you into your present reality, you hear the beautiful music of your soul and feel the gentle movement of the elevator. As the elevator doors open into your present life, you know you've just taken a sacred journey into your soul.

This time-tripping experiential journey you've just taken offers you unlimited opportunities to travel through time. You can take this trip through time into the multidimensional realms and realities of your soul as many times as you wish.

Every time you journey, you'll become aware of more information, and you'll understand more about your soul and how it travels through the energies of time.

# Universal Peace Project

—————————— ❧ ——————————

*Find peace within yourself, then join a group*
*of like-minded people and light-beings to share*
*vibrations of love, peace, joy, and harmony*
*throughout the world and the universe.*

Your inner journeys have brought you into a still, quiet, peaceful place within you—a special, sacred place filled with light—where you remember your soul's natural vibration—a vibration of light, love, joy, peace, and harmony.

Feel this vibration completely within yourself, with every part of your body, mind, and soul. Breathe it inside you; allow it to become part of you. The feeling is so filled with pure joy that words cannot adequately describe it, yet you completely feel it and know it within yourself.

This vibration of spiritual knowing and pure peace has so much joy and wisdom and beauty within it that it naturally desires to express itself. In a special, sacred place within you, within the center of your soul, the very core of your being, you have always, in every moment of your life, shared your vibrations with the world and the universe, even though you may not have been fully aware of it.

You have always come from a loving, white light place within your heart, mind, and soul. Because you are a spiritual being, born from a divine spark of love, you could not do otherwise, even though at times physical illusions may have prevented your clear seeing of the whole picture and of knowing the reasons for your experiences and actions. Yet your soul was ever-evolving, following its path of inner knowing directed by its inner source to its ultimate destiny—that of love and light.

Now that you've reawakened and remembered your spiritual awareness and the light within you, you know you can increase your power to share your vibrations of love, peace, joy, and harmony throughout the world and the universe by joining with others who have also awakened to this awareness.

Desiring to share your vibrations with the world, you draw into your life like-minded people—kindred spirits—who are also aware of their soul's natural vibrations, people who have awakened to their spiritual mission to share the light of their knowledge and the vibrations of love, joy, peace, and harmony in their own special, unique, individual way throughout the world.

As you join with this group—whether you're physically connected by geography or universally connected in mind and spirit—to share peace and love with everyone, you know that every soul who is now experiencing life on earth is truly a powerful, spiritual being of light, just as you are, and their spark of divine love is ever-present, sometimes waiting only for a way-shower—for your light to shine upon them to illuminate the light that is within them.

As these peaceful vibrations—both from within yourself and from like-minded people—surround you, you are joined by light-beings from the universe who have the same desire to share their vibrations of love, peace, joy, and harmony with the earth and throughout the universe, just as you do.

As you become connected with other spiritually-awakened people and light-beings through your soul's awareness, you know that your thoughts, feelings, and actions, and the way you express and manifest them in your life through all your many experiences, create vibrations of loving, peaceful energy everywhere as they simultaneously create beautiful, loving reverberations and ripples of peace and harmony throughout the earth and the universe.

# Mystical Moonlight

*Explore the effervescent energy of moonlight reflecting
on a still, quiet pool of water as you simultaneously
experience the light shimmering from the universe and
sparkling from within your soul, vibrating in harmony.*

It's a beautiful, warm, moonlit evening and you're enjoying a quiet stroll by a lake. Stopping to look at the reflection of the moon on the water, you notice how it shimmers with a luminescent light, almost as if it's alive. A calm, gentle breeze ripples across the surface, inspiring a magical, mystical sense of awareness within you.

Walking to the edge of the water, admiring the beauty of the reflection of moonlight on the water and enjoying the sense of harmony it brings forth within you, you notice how the light shimmers with an effervescent energy.

Stepping into the warm, shallow water, you feel the swirling effervescence gently bubbling around your feet. Bending down, you scoop up handfuls of the warm water, letting it run through your fingers, noticing the tingling in your hands.

As you splash the water over your face and body, bathing in the light from the moon reflecting on the water, you feel your hands and body become energized with the tingling effervescence of the water.

Joyfully, with carefree abandon, you play in the water. As you splash the water over your body and in circles all around you, you feel your body begin to tingle and vibrate with a sense of energy and vitality that you've experienced before, a long time ago when your spirit was free and filled with light. You realize you're bathing in the divine light of the universe—the light of your soul.

As this remembrance reawakens within you, you look up at the sky, at the infinite universe, and breathe in the light of the sparkling stars that combine their light with the light emanating and radiating from the moon.

You know this universal light reflects your soul's divine essence. You feel a beautiful, wonderful feeling of radiant health and harmony within your body, mind, and spirit, freeing you and opening you up even more to your true spiritual nature—that of a divine, powerful, spiritual being of light who has only taken up a temporary residence here on earth.

# A Shimmering Space

$\backsim$

*Take a brief journey "home" to feel and
experience the essence of your soul.*

You're in a beautiful garden of violet and purple flowers growing everywhere. Light shimmers all around the garden, illuminating a beautiful temple that you know is the home of your soul.

As you enter the temple, you feel an awe and reverence within you, deep within your soul. A violet sphere of light gently vibrates and shimmers all around you as you step into the place your soul calls home. Sunlight streams in through the stained-glass windows, reflecting the multicolored light of rainbows everywhere.

There's a hushed stillness within the temple of your soul that is very calming, soothing, and peaceful, and you sense something very ethereal in the violet light that is vibrating and shimmering all around you, as if the light is alive.

Inside this light that feels completely nurturing and peaceful, you become aware of your soul's light that resonates with the feelings of love, joy, peace, and harmony.

Within this light you see colors that go beyond what words can fully describe, a rainbow shimmering in the sky that shows you a scenic panorama of pictures. You know the images you see are the pictures of your soul, showing you scenes that resonate deep within you.

An energy that can only be called pure, unconditional love surrounds every part of you as it softly flows through you. You feel loved.

You feel a love and peace and joy that is completely in harmony with your energies, and you **know**—with every part of your being—that this is what "home" feels like.

# Center of the Sunrise

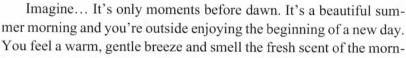

*You are a magical, spiritual being of light.*
*Travel into and beyond the center of the sunrise*
*and experience the dawning of the light within you.*

Sunrises hold a promise of a new and wonderful discovery—the dawn of a new beginning, the dawn of a new light beginning within you. Explore and experience the light within yourself as you travel in your mind into and beyond the center of the sunrise, as you completely remember your inner knowing and rediscover your spiritual knowledge. Somehow you know that if you travel beyond the sunrise, into the center of the sun, you'll find a magical treasure inside your soul.

Imagine... It's only moments before dawn. It's a beautiful summer morning and you're outside enjoying the beginning of a new day. You feel a warm, gentle breeze and smell the fresh scent of the morning air. You hear birds chirping in the distance; the sound is muted and pleasant as they welcome the dawn of a new day.

You know there's a beach nearby because you hear the sound of the waves, and you think you'd enjoy the sunrise even more if you were at the beach. As you walk toward the beach, you feel free and happy, enjoying the beginning of a brand-new day. Arriving at the beach, you feel the sand beneath your bare feet; it feels pleasantly warm and cushions you as you walk closer to the ocean.

Sitting on the beach, watching the waves as they gently touch the shore, you feel a wonderful sense of peace and harmony within you and all around you. Listening to the ebb and flow of the tide relaxes you completely. Breathing in deeply, you feel perfectly content, at one with yourself and with the world around you.

Looking up at the sky, across the water, you have a clear view of the horizon as the water seemingly touches the sky. You see a few clouds just above the horizon, and notice how they're tinged with the early colors of dawn.

Pale orange at first, then the pale orange blends into a beautiful mixture of coral and pink as the first rays of sunlight color the bottom of the clouds. It's almost as if the water is reflecting the color of the sunrise onto the clouds.

The beauty and misty softness of the colors inspire a sense of awe and wonderment inside you, and you realize you're seeing more than the colors of a new day; you're seeing the colors of a new beginning.

The sky is getting lighter. As the light from the sun begins to shine behind the clouds, you see the first rays of the sunrise begin to come over the horizon; you notice how the light is reflected and mirrored on the water. The light of this sunrise emanates a wonderful feeling of energy, and you sense this sunrise is very special; it's magical and has a mystical aura and ambiance about it.

Turning your face up to the sun, you breathe in the light. The warmth and light of the sun envelops you completely as you breathe it inside your mind and your body, as you feel it inside your heart. It fills you with pure energy and awareness. You feel your body and your mind—your heart and soul—vibrating in harmony with the warmth and light of the sun, with the energy of awareness.

As you feel and sense and experience the sunrise with every part of you, you feel drawn into the sunrise, knowing that you're ready to completely rediscover the magical, mystical power of your mind; you're ready to reawaken your spiritual awareness.

The early colors of dawn begin to change into the golden color of the sun, the color of knowledge. Somewhere within yourself, you realize that you are the colors of dawn. You are the colors of the sunrise.

Just as the water reflected the early colors of dawn onto the clouds and mirrored the beginning of the sunrise, you know that the sunrise mirrored within your mind is a reflection of your spiritual awareness, opening up within you, reawakening you to the knowledge and power you have within yourself.

The sunlight sparkles and shimmers on the water, reflecting the light. Centering your awareness into the sunrise, it becomes brighter and brighter, illuminating every part of your mind, filling your mind and your spirit with pure enlightenment.

You feel as if you're part of the light, as if you **are** the light, and somehow you know you're seeing the light of your soul. You know the sunrise is within you and that you are the sunrise. The light grows brighter and brighter, expanding and radiating everywhere, emanating rays of light and wisdom.

As you're enjoying the rays and warmth and light of the sun, you feel the light and warmth spread throughout your entire body, mind, and spirit, flowing into and through every part of your being.

The sun is above the horizon now, and as the sun continues to rise in the sky, you rise with it—higher and higher. The feeling is exhilarating, and you feel more alive and awake and aware than you've ever felt before.

There's a special, spiritual place you know of, a magical place you've just remembered is beyond the colors of dawn, beyond the colors of the sunrise. As you go into and through and beyond the light of the sunrise, you enter that special and most magical place within yourself.

It feels as if you're coming home, as if you're returning to yourself. You know you've been here before in this sacred place inside your soul. You've always known the way to this most special and magical place.

You see the sun beginning to rise in the center of yourself and you know you're completely opening up the magical power of your mind, the mystical power of your spiritual awareness. As you become aware of your true spiritual essence, a pure white light—a light brighter than the sunrise—enters into every part of your mind. You notice how the light vibrates and dances around you, and you begin to feel it vibrate within you.

You feel this light, this magical energy of spiritual knowledge vibrating inside you—inside your body, your mind, your heart, and your soul. You experience feelings of awe and wonder and pure joy as you completely open yourself up to the light and allow this empowering energy of spiritual awareness and enlightenment to enter inside you, knowing it has always been part of you.

This pure white light opens your awareness to the truth of your spiritual essence. As the light becomes brighter and brighter within you, you become more and more aware of your inner essence and your spiritual knowledge—knowledge that is infinite and goes beyond what words can describe.

You know this light is the light of your soul—the light that shines within you, the light of your spiritual essence vibrating all around you and within you.

As you breathe in the pure and positive energy of the light, you fully absorb the spiritual energy within yourself, knowing that your spiritual enlightenment is completely opening up inside you as you become more aware and awake than ever before.

As you accept the light that is radiating from within the center of the sunrise, from within the center of your being—your soul—you become fully aware of your true spiritual nature and you know that *you are the universal essence of light that shines upon the earth*.

The light within you becomes brighter as the sun continues to rise. Your spiritual knowledge and the awareness of your true nature is interwoven with the rays of sunshine, with the colors of a new day, a new beginning. Your inner awareness becomes clearer and brighter at every moment as you experience and enjoy the sunrise, as you experience enlightenment within your heart, mind, and soul.

You feel completely connected with the light of the sun and you know, somewhere deep within yourself, that the source of light from the sun is the same source your soul draws from. You feel yourself becoming the essence of your spirit—radiating and emanating the same golden rays of light you're receiving and experiencing from the sun.

Enjoy and explore the light within you as you rediscover your true spiritual essence, as you completely open up the magical, mystical power of your mind.

You see a golden sun ray that emanates from the sunrise, a golden sun ray that emanates from you. You notice how the sun ray originates from the sun and from you, and how it travels from its source to gently touch the earth and light the way of a beautiful new day.

You notice how this sun ray sparkles on the water and shines on the beach where you watched the dawn begin, where you enjoyed the beginning of the sunrise. Become part of that golden sun ray and travel with it onto the beach where you watched the dawning of the light within you.

You're sitting on the beach again, and you see that the sun is completely above the horizon, above the clouds. The colors are different now; the clouds that reflected the early colors of dawn now reflect the color of gold, the color of the sun, and the color of knowledge. The sky is a very bright blue, and even as you look at the clouds that are golden, they change to a pure white as if they've absorbed the light of the sunrise.

Looking above you at the sun that is still rising in the sky, you feel the aura and atmosphere of light all around you, and you know the sun is vibrating with universal light and energy. You feel the radiant light of the sun shining brightly overhead, its rays warming the air, creating its own special ambiance.

You feel the ambiance all around you—the sun is sharing its radiant light and perfect warmth; the rays of light are warming your body, mind, heart, and soul. You feel your soul opening up completely to the light—to the light of knowledge. You feel every thought in your mind opening up and becoming more aware.

You look over the water and notice how the sunlight sparkles and shimmers, mirroring and reflecting the light from the sun. And you know the light of your soul shines brightly within you and is mirrored and reflected in the world around you.

You feel the warmth of the sun and the gentle breeze as it softly caresses you. You smell the scent of the morning air and hear the sound of birds chirping in the distance as they welcome the light— the dawn of a new day.

You smile up at the sun, knowing you've remembered the magic inside your soul and rediscovered your spiritual knowledge within yourself on the journey you've just taken beyond the center of the sunrise.

# The Joy is in the Journey

The inner journey continues...

As you continue to journey into yourself—to see and know all that is within your heart, mind, and soul—and you open yourself up to your inner spiritual knowing and expand your awareness, reaching above the horizons of your physical world into the universe, you'll become aware of the many joys and riches and treasures your spirit offers you.

You'll discover the opening up of your awareness is like the dawn of a new beginning that offers a promise of many new and wonderful adventures and discoveries. You'll see your spiritual awareness reflected and mirrored in every experience in your life as you journey upon this path you're now traveling—a magical, mystical path in your mind that leads you into the light of your soul.

You'll see and actualize your spiritual self—that very special, sacred part of you—that is reflected in every aspect of your day-to-day activities, in every thought, feeling, and experience you have in your life, and you'll reawaken to your true spiritual nature, to the energy essence of yourself—the universal light-being that you truly are.

Travel lightly on your journeys. Remember that the joy is in the journey.

# Whispers Beyond
# the Rainbow

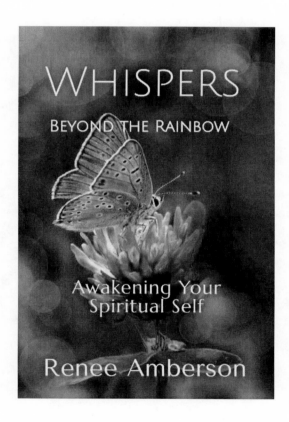

# Introduction

*A magical rainbow journey invites you to look for the
light within yourself and reawaken your spiritual self.*

Once upon a time, somewhere inside a dream, a rainbow whispered
to me, inviting me to follow a rainbow path into spiritual awakening.
I woke up to my soul's knowledge—to the awareness of my true spiritual nature.

One morning, I woke to the sound of rain tapping gently on my
window. The sun was shining, so I looked out the window and saw a
beautiful rainbow shimmering in the sunlight and heard a whisper
asking if I wanted to travel through the rainbow and explore the colors.

The energies of a rainbow are very spiritual, so I decided to follow my dream and journey through the light of a magical, mystical
rainbow. **Whispers** shares my rainbow journey and is based on some
of the meditations in **Inner Journeys** (Echoes of Light ~ Book One).

We're all travelers through this earth experience we call life. I'm
glad your journey has led you to this book. As we journey through
our experiences, it's important to remember who we truly are: Powerful, spiritual beings of light.

Because our souls vibrate to and resonate with the colors and energies of a rainbow, I invite you to travel a more-than-magical rainbow journey into your soul as you look for the light within yourself.

I'd like to think you will read **Whispers** as a gentle meditation, pausing to reflect on your thoughts and feelings when something resonates with you, to allow images, thoughts, and feelings to open inside you as you travel inside your own spiritual awareness.

I hope **Whispers** will inspire you to experience your own rainbow journey—to travel a rainbow path into your soul. It is also my sincere hope that you will experience the joy of reawakening your spiritual self.

## A Spiritual Quest...

*You are a powerful,*
*spiritual being of light.*

*Your soul is a divine spark of*
*light, waiting until you are ready*
*to awaken and become fully aware*
*of your true spiritual nature.*

*Journey through magical, mystical*
*worlds of inner images as your spirit*
*travels on wings of light into special,*
*sacred places inside your soul.*

*Listen to the whispers and look beyond*
*the rainbow to enter a multidimensional*
*realm of knowledge and remembrance.*

# Part One

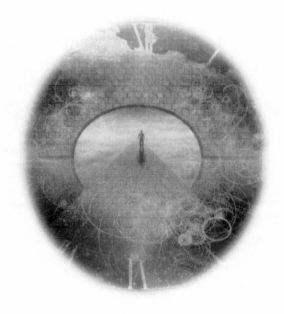

## *Whispers*

# Chapter One

———— ∽ ————

## The Rainbow Path

*Once upon a dream…*

Still half asleep, I listened to the rain patter gently on the glass of the open window. The sound was lulling and soothing, comforting and relaxing.

I felt as if I was dreaming, as if I was inside a magical, wonderful dream. As the soft, steady rhythm of the rain continued to gently tap on the window, I felt peaceful and quiet within myself.

Thinking I should get up and close the window, I noticed it was nearly dawn. The sun was beginning to rise, spreading its light over the earth. I thought this was curious—that the sun could be seen through the clouds.

I rose to close the window and looking up at the sky, I saw the most beautiful rainbow I've ever seen. It was shimmering in the light reflected from the sun, radiating sparkles of rainbow-colored light everywhere.

It seemed to surround me like a perfect dome that touched the earth and the sky. The colors of the rainbow were vibrant and pure, a shimmering spectrum of colors that blended into one another, vibrating perfectly in tune with each other, creating harmony within my mind and my soul.

I wondered how a rainbow could appear in the sky when it was still raining and the sun wasn't fully above the horizon or clearly visible through the soft, misty clouds and decided I must be dreaming. The clouds began to clear—becoming iridescent, then luminous, and then transparent—and the rainbow seemed to open up in the sunshine, showing me a path inside its colors.

"Follow your dream," the rainbow said.

If I was dreaming, I thought to myself, then maybe I could fly up into and through this shimmering rainbow and follow the path to see where it would lead me. It sounded like a wonderful thing to do and I decided to follow this dream.

I heard the voice whisper again in my mind, somewhere inside my dream. "Would you like to take a wonderful journey into a magical, mystical place where you can follow a rainbow path to open up the true reality of your physical world and explore the multidimensionality of your soul, to remember and rediscover all the knowledge you have within you as you awaken to your spiritual self?"

"Yes," I said, and I was inside the color red at the bottom of the rainbow. I wondered what I'd find inside each color.

# Chapter Two

⤫

## *Spiritual Search*

As I entered the color red inside the rainbow, I felt as if I was wandering through a softly-swirling misty maze—a shimmering space—looking for something special inside me. I wasn't quite sure what I was really looking for, but knew I'd recognize it immediately when I found it. I knew I was on a journey in search of my soul, looking for my true spiritual essence.

My search was also about finding my truth, and the meaning and purpose in my life. Somewhere inside my soul, I felt as if something special was missing in my life, that I had somehow misplaced it, yet knew I could find it—that I could remember it.

Just like the rainbow had offered, I felt as if I was beginning a wonderful adventure that would show me the way to my spiritual knowledge. I began to look inside my mind, peering into almost-forgotten dreams and misty memories, searching for an image, a clue, a doorway, or a window—a way to remember.

Then I thought of the window in my dream that had opened into the light of a shimmering sunrise. I began to get clearer on what I was searching for. I was looking for the answer to something I'd pondered about and puzzled over for many years, perhaps many lifetimes.

I wanted to know who I really am and why I'm here. I was looking for the realness in my life, for the meaning and purpose, and what I was meant to do with my life.

But I knew it went much deeper than that. I was searching for my spiritual essence, for the knowledge and truth inside me. I wanted to awaken my spiritual self, to see through the illusions I'd enshrouded myself in. I wanted to see through my physical nature into the true reality of my spiritual nature. I was looking for myself—my soul. But where was that to be found?

I quieted the chatter in my conscious mind and went within the stillness of myself to meditate, knowing that the answers I was searching for were there. But what did the rainbow have to do with all of this? I wondered. I sensed that the complete awareness of my true spiritual nature could be found somewhere inside the rainbow. Perhaps this was the treasure at the end of the rainbow I'd always heard about.

When my search was complete, I could reunite with myself, encircling the essence of my soul around me. I knew it would feel as if I was being embraced with the gentleness and love and joy of my spiritual self, as if I was coming home. I knew that when I'd found myself, it would be like giving myself a very special gift. I don't know how I knew all this; I just *knew* that I knew.

And when I'd found what I've been searching for—my spiritual self—I'd be able to remember all my spiritual knowledge. I also knew that I'd be able to share my knowledge, and to express the pure energy of my soul in every emotion and experience in my life.

I saw a vision of the light of my soul shining and shimmering brightly, like the light of a sunrise. I was eager to continue the journey on this rainbow path that would guide me into my soul. With this thought, I began to rise into the color orange.

## Chapter Three

—————— ✍ ——————

## *Inner Light*

I seemed to be in a classroom, but I was the only student there. I sat down at a desk and waited for a teacher to appear. I noticed a large, white candle in the center of the room and sensed that this was a meditation class.

Listening to the thoughts inside me, I intuitively knew that I was my own teacher and that no one would appear who could teach me anything I didn't already know within my soul or that I couldn't learn for myself through my experiences.

It was then that I noticed the candle had sparkled into a flame—that my thoughts had somehow caused this to occur—and I heard a voice whisper inside my mind. I knew it was my inner voice—my rainbow voice—and I listened to what it said to me.

"It's time for you to know that what you previously thought of as three separate selves—your inner self, your higher self, and your soul—are all one and the same.

"Your energy essence—your soul—begins within your feelings. Meditating on the flame of the candle will help you raise your awareness above physical energies by first focusing on inner aspects of energy within yourself, then raising your awareness into higher vibrations above yourself, and then centering your attention on the energies around yourself into the essence of yourself."

It sounded like a wonderful meditation, a way to blend my physical consciousness with my inner feelings, to remember my spiritual knowledge, to become completely aware of my soul, and to bring this awareness into every part of my life. I continued to listen to my inner voice, to the teacher within me.

"Focusing on these levels of awareness will put you in touch with the spiritual energies and expressions of your inner self and your higher self, and show you how to tune into the energy vibrations of your soul and your true spiritual self—into the light of knowledge."

I was beginning to understand how these levels of awareness were interwoven, and how they all worked together, and was beginning to feel a sense of oneness with myself, and I hadn't even begun to meditate yet.

My inner voice seemed to acknowledge the knowing inside my mind, then continued as if it—I?—knew that I wanted more clarity, to better understand myself on all levels.

"The center of the flame represents your inner self and your feelings. The flame of the candle represents your higher self. The aura around the candle, which is the energy essence of the flame, represents your soul.

"As you focus individually on the separate parts, you'll become aware of and in tune with these vibrations of energy within yourself and you'll know how to interweave them, to bring them together into a unified whole.

"Begin by looking into the center of the flame. Sense the energy that emanates from within the center of the flame. Feel the energy that emanates from within you. Become in tune with the vibrations of your inner self and your inner feelings.

"Go within the center of your awareness, and feel the energy vibrations that begin to form your spiritual essence. Become aware of the light and life within you that begins inside your feelings and radiates and expands all around you."

I could feel shimmers of warmth beginning to spread within myself, from within the center of my being. I was resonating with the energies of my inner self. I continued to meditate a while longer, to get more in tune with my inner self and in touch with my feelings.

I heard my rainbow voice again. "Look at the flame of the candle; begin to feel and sense the energy vibrations of your higher self. As you become in tune with your higher levels of energy and awareness, you expand into the vibrations of your higher self and the knowledge you have within you."

I felt as if there was a book opening up inside me and wondered why that thought had appeared in my mind. Probably because books contain knowledge, I answered myself. At the same time, I felt as if knowledge was literally pouring into my mind, reminding me of what I already knew on both an inner and a more aware, higher level within myself.

I could feel my awareness beginning to glow and radiate in rhythm and harmony with the flame of the candle as if I was part of the light—yet knowing at the same time that I *was* the light—again feeling that wonderful, shimmering sense of warmth and resonance spread through my entire body and my mind, encircling my heart and soul at the same time.

"Look around the flame of the candle at the aura of energy around the flame," my inner voice—my teacher within—said. The voice was clearer and louder than before. When I'd first heard it and began to listen, it was only a whisper I could barely hear above the chatter in my mind.

"The aura is the energy essence of the flame, encircling itself. Notice the sparkles around the outside of the flame, how they dance in rhythm and harmony with the flame, with the essence of your inner self and your higher self. Notice how the aura shimmers and moves, how it's alive with energy.

"Feel the energy that emanates from your soul. As you become aware of your energy essence, you feel a warm, flowing, fluid movement begin to vibrate inside you—inside your feelings, bringing them together with your spiritual knowledge and blending them with the awareness of your soul."

I had already begun to experience this vibration earlier in the meditation. I smiled to myself; I had always known how to blend my energies together, but had forgotten until now that I innately and intuitively knew how to do this. I also knew that this was a spiritual birthright of every soul.

"As you feel your energy essence glowing within you and radiating all around you, you become more aware of your spiritual energies that transcend physical energies. You become more aware that you are a spiritual being and that you are the essence of light.

"Completely encircle yourself with the pure energy vibration of your soul. Feel it radiating from within the center of yourself, opening up and expanding inside you, then radiating out and vibrating all around you, forming your aura—your essence. As you become more aware of the essence of your soul, the flame becomes brighter, and the aura around the flame sparkles and shimmers with increased energy."

I felt a powerful energy and awareness welling up inside me, spreading and flowing within me, from within the center of my being, rising up above me and vibrating in harmony all around me, resonating with every part of my body, my mind, and my soul. I could feel it vibrating warmly in my heart and radiating all around me in sparkles and shimmers of light.

I couldn't find the words to describe it, though it felt familiar and I knew I'd experienced it before in some of the spiritual experiences in my life when I'd truly been in touch with my soul. And there were other times when I'd felt and experienced this feeling in another part of my awareness, somewhere inside a special, sacred place in my soul.

I continued to meditate, feeling the essence of my soul vibrating in perfect harmony and synchronicity with my inner feelings and my spiritual knowledge. I knew that what I had just experienced within the energies of my inner self, my higher self, and my soul had brought me into a oneness and harmony with myself.

I no longer felt separate from myself. I was a completely spiritual being, whole within myself. I felt as if I'd found the missing pieces of myself and brought them together.

I knew how special and spiritual this meditation was, and I also knew that in every moment of my life, I could instantly attain this level of mind again—this complete spiritual awareness and together-ness with myself—at any time, no matter where I was or what I was doing.

And every time I did this—on a conscious, more aware level—I would become even more aware of and in tune with my inner self, my higher self, and my soul, and I'd be able to bring them closer together, to connect them more in harmony. I knew that this was a very special gift from the rainbow, given to myself.

I was resonating with the rainbow and remembering my feelings when I'd first entered the rainbow in my dream, when I felt the rainbow all around me and within me, and I'd become a rainbow of colors, expanding both inward and outward in a shimmering essence of light. It seemed that my dream was much more than a dream; it was becoming more and more real, and I felt as if I was becoming more awake and aware.

I had a sense—a real feeling of knowing—that my inner teacher was more than she appeared to be. She was more than a rainbow; she was a way-shower, a light-being from the universe, shining her light and radiance upon the earth.

Maybe I'm a spiritual sun ray, I thought to myself, smiling as I imagined myself shining and shimmering my light upon the earth.

My voice continued speaking and this time I really heard it inside my soul. "By doing this meditation, you raised your awareness and your spiritual energy vibrations, blending them with all the experiences in your life. At the same time, you began to see through the illusions of your physical reality into the true awareness of your soul."

Where do we go from here? I wondered, beginning to feel like a free spirit.

My voice answered, "You can expand your awareness even further, into the multidimensionality of your soul."

Like a butterfly that emerges from its cocoon and spreads its wings to fly—to soar into the sky, the universe and beyond, I mused.

"As you become more aware of and in tune with the energy vibrations of your inner self, your higher self, and your soul, you become aware of the true nature of all your experiences; you become aware of the true nature of your spirituality and you reawaken your spiritual self."

Suddenly I heard the most beautiful music and wondered where it was coming from. It sounded like a celestial chorus singing inside my body, my heart, my mind, and my soul.

The words echoed in my mind, repeating themselves through the simultaneous vibrations of my inner self, my higher self, and my soul, blending perfectly in harmony—into my spiritual self—the essence of me.

I'd always sensed within me that my feelings, my knowledge, and my soul were one and the same, but could never seem to bring them all together until now. It was so wonderful to be a whole person, not scattered or separate from myself.

This dream—if it was a dream—was beginning to feel very real; it was getting better all the time. I felt as if I was waking up inside the dream, inside my awareness. I was beginning to recognize, and to really know, that the rainbow voice was my own inner voice.

I wanted more knowledge. I wanted to know more about myself, about my soul. With this thought, I began to rise into the color yellow inside the rainbow. I remembered reading somewhere that the color yellow was the color of knowledge.

# Chapter Four

— ✑ —

## *Light Library*

Maybe I could go to the library and find a book that would give me more knowledge, I thought to myself. The image of that thought showed me a spiral stairway shimmering with light.

Placing my foot on the bottom step, I felt a gentle wave of energy flow through me. Traveling up the stairs, the vibration of energy softly radiated upward from my feet through my entire body.

I began to feel as if I was floating a few inches above the steps, gliding through emanations of energy, weightless and free, flowing into higher realms of light. The top of the stairs were shrouded in a soft, white mist. As I entered the mist, it cleared, showing a vibrant path shimmering with light.

Following the path, I felt the pure white light vibrating gently all around me, filling me with a wonderful feeling of peace and harmony.

A few steps ahead, I saw a building that was illuminated with the shimmering white light. The building emanated and radiated a special kind of energy that resonated with my soul.

The light welcomed me within. Entering the library, I saw that it was created entirely with the vibrant energy of the light itself. Light was everywhere. Rays of universal light flowed in through the open windows.

Vibrations of light formed the floors and the walls. Beams of sparkling energy supported the arched ceiling; in the center was a domed skylight through which I could see the light of the universe.

A magical aura surrounded the library; ethereal energies of pure awareness softly reverberated through the vast array of books.

A hushed stillness echoed within the library even as it shimmered with energy, with the knowledge contained in the books that filled the shelves and lined the walls. As I listened quietly, I heard the books talk in whispers of wisdom and murmurs of mystical knowledge. The rows of books appeared to be endless, as if they went on forever.

Walking through the aisles and the alcoves, I saw books on every subject imaginable and knew that this library contained all the knowledge that had ever been written or recorded, in all the world and the entire universe, since the beginning of time, since the beginning of thought.

Running my fingers over the titles of the books, I felt a shimmer of energy go through me and discovered that I could read them within my mind. The books were written in a universal language that I understood easily, just by touching the books or looking at the pictures on the covers. The words and their images danced into my mind, creating a symphony of sound vibrations, and within the music and the melody, I understood the knowledge inside each book.

Continuing to walk through the library, exploring the light energies of knowledge, I noticed another stairway with seven steps that vibrated with a light more dazzling, more brilliant than the light that surrounded the open entrance to the library.

The light shimmered and sparkled with energy, as if it was alive. I sensed a sacred feeling about this light; it seemed to contain an essence within itself.

The vibrations emanating from this light were filled with images of color that had shape and substance. It looked like a beautiful blur of rainbow colors in a gentle wave of motion, forming into ever-changing transparent prisms of light.

Looking into the light, I experienced an emotion that went beyond words and thoughts, and I knew that I was about to enter a very sacred space inside my soul. More than anything else, I wanted to be part of that light.

I wanted to rush into the light, to become the essence of the light, yet felt I might disturb it if I rushed, so I waited, respectfully and reverently. The light opened up and invited me in, just as the light at the entrance to the library had welcomed me within. Stepping into the light, I was filled with a feeling of awe and wonderment and pure joy.

Each step of the stairway vibrated in harmony with the colors of a rainbow. Walking slowly, thoughtfully, up the stairs, I paused on every step—feeling the energy, hearing the unique vibration, the tone and hue and experience of each color.

Ascending the stairs and absorbing the colors within my body, my mind, and my feelings—within every part of me in perfect harmony, I became more and more aware of my soul.

As my awareness expanded, I knew I was traveling a stairway that would lead me into the true essence of myself. As I experienced my awareness flowing into and through the vibrations of the rainbow, I felt as if I was flying through the energies of muted sounds and colors.

Reaching the top of the stairs, I saw that the higher echelon of the library was a loft that contained the written records of every soul's existence and I knew—with an absolute knowing—that these books vibrated with a light that was unique to every soul and that they could only be opened and read by that particular soul.

In the center of the loft, I saw a table with an open book and a lamp that glowed with a luminous light. Next to the table was a comfortable chair. I walked over to the table and looked at the book.

It seemed that the library had been waiting for me to discover it, and the open book had been waiting to be read by me. Knowing that this book was about my soul, I looked at the chapter title the book was opened to—**Follow Your Dream: A Rainbow Path Into Awakening**.

As I read the words, they began to vibrate on the page, then to shimmer with a soft glow of light, radiating into rays of energy which formed images that swirled into my thoughts and sparkled into pictures, opening a special kind of knowing within my mind. Touching the words, my hand began to vibrate with energy.

I realized how very special this book was. Picking it up, I settled comfortably in the chair. Holding the open book in my hands, my body began to vibrate with energy.

I felt as if I was being drawn inside the pages of the book as the words vibrated and resonated in my mind, moving in rhythm and harmony with the flow of spiritual and universal energy. I felt as if a gentle current of energy was flowing through me, opening up and releasing a higher awareness within. As the energy continued to softly flow through me, I knew that my spiritual awareness was opening up inside me, beginning to surge and soar through every part of my body, mind, and soul.

This is so wonderful, so magical, I thought, smiling to myself—a special smile that I understood deep inside my soul. Hugging the book close to my heart, I knew I'd found a very special treasure—a book that reveals all my spiritual knowledge, a book that shows me the secrets of my soul.

As I read the chapter title again, the words formed an image that drew complete and detailed pictures in my mind. I could see a rainbow path shimmering with light. I touched the pictures in the book—the pictures in my mind—feeling the texture of the images. The pictures were solid. The scene was real; it wasn't an image that disappeared when I blinked my eyes.

*The words formed real pictures*. When I read the words, they formed pictures that came to life—three-dimensional images that vibrated from the pages into my awareness, into my physical reality—resonating with an energy source that was inspired by the words on the pages.

The book was energy in motion and the words magically transported me inside my rainbow dream. I was there, inside the picture; I was really there. Looking around myself, I saw and felt and experienced everything there was to see and feel and experience.

I saw the candle. I saw a magical forest with a tree that talked to me, and a shimmering white cloud in an azure-blue sky that transported me everywhere I wanted to go. I saw a music box that played beautiful music inside my soul when I opened it. I watched the birth of a butterfly as it emerged from its chrysalis and I became the butterfly as it flew somewhere over the rainbow and soared into the universe.

Then I was sitting on a beach watching the dawn of a new day, enjoying the light of the sun and I traveled a magical sun ray beyond the spectrum of the sunrise into the light of my soul. Beyond the sunrise, there was a bridge that shimmered with a beautiful rainbow light.

The book was filled with every experience I'd ever had or will have, and yet I knew I could write and rewrite the pages and paragraphs in any way that I chose.

As I looked through the pages and read the words that had already been written, my experiences came to life and I completely understood—with a clarity and knowing that went beyond words—why they had happened and why I'd chosen to experience them.

I felt—with every part of myself, with every part of my awareness—the events and emotions inside my experiences as the words drew detailed and descriptive images and scenes within my mind.

The book was timeless as it portrayed the pictures of my soul—the essence of my spirit—as it spoke to me of the events and emotions in my life, and showed me all the many, various aspects of all my experiences in every time frame—past, present, and future—and in every dimension of being, in every realm of my awareness. The book showed me the true reality of me, the true multidimensionality of my soul.

I began to wonder if this dream was my real life. It seemed they were both one and the same. It also seemed that every part of my dream was opening me up to an increased level of awareness and understanding of my spiritual self as I traveled higher and higher into and through the colors of the rainbow.

I was beginning to feel a bit overwhelmed with all the experiences in the book and the awareness that was opening up inside me. I decided to go for a walk through nature to ponder my thoughts and to absorb my experiences within me when I heard my rainbow voice in my mind.

"You've come a long way from when you first entered the rainbow in your dream to follow your path to awakening your spiritual self. Are you ready to continue on the rainbow path that leads you within to truly become a free spirit and to find your own special place in the sun where you can be the spiritual person that you really are and always were?"

I nodded yes, beginning to flow into the color green, knowing that my physical self was really a mirror of my spiritual self, and that I was ready to more fully awaken within myself.

# Chapter Five

❧

## *Magical Forest*

Arriving in the color green, I saw a magical forest surrounded with a softly-swirling white mist, or perhaps it was sunbeams—rays of light—and they only appeared to be misty because of the clouds floating above and through the forest. Maybe I was ready to see through the mist, into the clear light of my soul, I thought to myself.

The scene was enchanting, like something out of a movie and yet I knew it was very real. I sensed it was a special, sacred place where I knew I could become even more aware of my true essence—my real self—and I could rediscover and reclaim all the joys and treasures and gifts that my spiritual self has to offer me.

I remembered when I rose through the colors inside the rainbow and began to rediscover the magical, mystical secrets of my soul, and now I was ready to travel further along the path that led me within. I knew the rainbow was there in the sunshine, somewhere.

The forest beckoned me, inviting me to experience the peace I felt within myself and to feel connected with the earth, to appreciate the beauty of nature and to experience the harmony of the earth with the universe, the harmony of my physical self with my spiritual self.

I wanted to experience again the wonder and awe of the natural world all around me as I began to fully open up and explore the spiritual world within me. Deep inside myself, I knew that I was part of that special connection between the earth and the universe, and I wanted to feel that again.

The day was filled with the quiet sounds of nature. The light from the sun shone all around me. I could feel and hear the gentle breeze as it touched me and moved softly through the leaves of the trees in the forest ahead of me. Walking toward the trees, I felt the warmth and energy of the sun and I began to experience the sense of aliveness and vibrancy that being in nature brings me.

Breathing in deeply, I felt the pure, clean air circulate through my lungs, revitalizing and rejuvenating every part of me. As this physical/universal energy flowed through my body and my mind, touching my heart and my spirit, I felt lighter and happier.

Breathing out, I let go of all my cares and worries. I could feel them slip away as I enjoyed this beautiful day, this wonderful walk through nature.

Following the rainbow path that led me within, I entered the forest. The sunshine sparkled and shimmered through the leaves at the top of the trees, creating patterns and playing with shafts of light on the forest floor. I noticed how intricate the patterns were, and how they were constantly moving and changing. I compared them to my experiences, and how my experiences were constantly changing in harmony with my thoughts and feelings, moving in rhythm with my mind's awareness.

Walking through the open, airy forest, I felt as if I was walking on a soft bed of earth. I noticed how quiet it was inside the forest, and how peaceful it was. I began to enter a meditative frame of mind—a special, serene place within myself where I felt completely comfortable and natural.

I saw a circular clearing up ahead and the sunlight beckoned me forth, welcoming me. I knew I'd been here before, inside this sacred place within myself—this sacred place inside my thoughts and dreams.

I felt perfectly at home and centered within myself, in tune with nature, as I walked slowly into the clearing, completely enjoying the feelings of peace and harmony within myself and all around me.

Beams of light shimmered through the treetops. I gazed up at the sun shining brightly in the sky. The mists I'd seen earlier had dissipated and disappeared.

I heard a tree calling to me and walked to the side of the clearing. Gently touching the tree, and hugging it as if it was an old and very dear friend, I sat quietly on the soft ground for a few minutes next to it. Then leaning back against the tree, I closed my eyes, listening to my thoughts and watching their images move in my mind.

The gentle breeze created a light, musical sound that vibrated in harmony within my mind as the wind blew softly through the leaves of the tree. The leaves whispered in the wind and through my mind, sharing the secrets of nature with me.

Somehow I knew I could communicate with the tree, and I listened as it told me about its connection with the earth and the universe, about how its roots are connected to the earth as its branches reach outward and upward to touch the light of the sky, and even higher, to embrace the universe.

The tree spoke to me of the harmony that is within all of nature, the harmony that the earth and the universe share with nature, the harmony that I share between my physical self and my spiritual self, the harmony that exists between my inner and outer worlds.

The tree told me that the universe is within me and that I am the universe, expressing myself—my spiritual nature—in physical form, and that as I reach outward and upward, I become more connected with the energies of the universe, in harmony with my physical experiences on earth.

After a while, I opened my eyes. Looking up at the sky, I saw a few shimmering white clouds floating leisurely by, and I noticed how blue and expansive the sky was. It seemed to go on forever, beyond the horizon into the universe and even farther than that into infinity. I wondered what it would be like to float on one of those puffy white clouds.

The sky had an ethereal quality—a magical, mystical essence that I couldn't describe with words—a majesty that I've known before but haven't experienced for a long time. Breathing in deeply, I absorbed every part of the blueness within myself; the color filled me with a wonderful sense of inner peace and awareness, a sense of knowing within my mind.

As I breathed in the blueness of the sky, I felt a more aware level of communication opening inside me between my inner self and my spiritual self, between my conscious mind and my subconscious mind. I knew I could really listen to and hear myself on all levels of my awareness, and that I could also tune into nature and commune with all of nature. I felt at one with nature and at one within myself.

Standing up, I felt as if I could reach up through the sky and touch the light of the universe. Stretching my arms upward in an open embrace toward the sky, I felt a magical surge of energy and awareness inside me, knowing that I am part of the earth and the universe, in harmony with the physical world around me and the spiritual world within me.

I sensed how infinite those worlds really are and I began to rediscover how infinite I really am. I began to recognize that I am a powerful, spiritual being. I began to remember the awareness I have within me, within my mind and my soul. I began to feel my spiritual nature opening up inside me, expanding into the universe.

I decided to continue walking, to explore everything I saw, to totally experience and understand both the world around me and the world within me. I moved in rhythm and harmony with my mind's awareness that was opening up more completely.

Reaching the edge of the forest, I entered a field of flowers growing wild and free in a meadow. Walking through them, I sensed how truly alive the flowers are; I sensed how special and magical they are.

Light flickered softly in the center of each flower. A gentle wind was blowing, as soft as a whisper. I watched as the flowers seemed to dance in harmony with the gentle breeze—radiating sparkles and shimmers of light.

Breathing in their wonderful fragrance, I sensed their inner essence and became aware of how they're connected to both the earth and the universe, just as I am. I became aware of their natural harmony with the world around them and the world within them, just as

I sensed and experienced the natural harmony of my physical self with my spiritual self.

The flowers were vibrantly alive, flowing with the natural energy of life and their inner essence, and I knew I was even more vibrantly alive, flowing with the energy of life and the essence of my spirituality.

Ahead of me, the meadow turned into a gently-sloping valley. As I looked into the valley, I saw how green and healthy and vibrant and beautiful everything was. I saw a mountain in the distance, rising up majestically into the sky. The sun radiated sparkles of light from a softly-winding stream of water in the center of the valley and I heard the sound of a waterfall.

Stopping to listen to the sound, I knew, as if I'd been here before, that the waterfall was hidden just beyond the bushes and large rocks that I saw on my right. Walking that way, I could smell the water and almost see a rainbow. Smiling to myself, I knew that the rainbow I saw in my mind was real and that I'd found the path that leads me within to my true spiritual self.

Parting the bushes, I saw a magnificent waterfall gushing with life as it cascaded into a gentle, quiet pool beneath. I felt the misty spray gently touch my face with its magical rainbow aura. Every drop of water sparkled as it caught the sunlight and reflected a beautiful, shimmering rainbow. It was like the waterfall was shimmering with light.

I followed the footpath down through the lush, flowering bushes to where the waterfall entered the clear, sparkling pool. I looked up into the azure-blue sky, seeing the soft wisps of a few billowy white clouds floating leisurely above me, and felt the warmth of the sun gently caressing my face and skin.

Looking down at the still, calm pool of water, I saw how the sunshine sparkled and shimmered on the quiet, tranquil pond, reflecting the blueness of the sky and the white wispiness of the clouds. Looking into the clear, sparkling water, I felt a gentle breeze ripple over the water, softly caressing it.

Kneeling down to run my fingers through the water, and looking into the gently-rippling pond, I saw more than the reflection of my physical self on the mirror-like surface of the water. Shimmering in the water was the essence of my inner, spiritual self, moving around and through my image in gentle ripples.

I noticed how the water mirrored and reflected the sky above me and I recognized that my physical self is really a mirror of my spiritual self, and that all my experiences in every dimension of reality and awareness reflect the knowledge I have within me. At the same time, I remembered and realized the infinite reality of my soul and that my soul mirrors both the earth and the universe.

And I knew that the reality of my physical experiences goes much deeper than my conscious mind, much farther than the physical world. Below the surface, and all around me in every experience, thought, and feeling, my inner awareness—my spiritual self waits— ever so quietly to be recognized, to be heard.

As I began to more fully open up both my physical consciousness and my spiritual awareness, I heard my inner voice whispering to me in my thoughts and feelings, and through my dreams and experiences. As I listened, I knew I could feel and become completely aware of all the vibrations of all my experiences as I traveled through them, following my rainbow path that leads me within to my spiritual self.

# Chapter Six

———————— ✥ ————————

## *Clearing Clouds*

Am I awake or am I dreaming? I wondered, rising up into the color blue inside the rainbow. I was outside on a beautiful, sunny day, enjoying the gentle breeze and the warmth and light of the sunshine.

Looking up at the sky, I saw a few shimmering white clouds floating leisurely by. I noticed how blue and expansive the sky was, just like it had been in the clearing in the forest when I'd wondered what it would be like to float on one of those puffy white clouds.

Blue, I remembered somewhere in my mind, was the color of communication. Maybe I could talk to the cloud, to see what it has to say. Or maybe I could communicate with the sky, to open a universal channel of awareness and clarity.

I again wondered, this time with more intent, what it would be like to float leisurely through the sky on a light, fluffy cloud. Would it change my perceptions or my perspective of things? Would it help clear some cloudiness in my mind, and open up a higher understanding?

My thoughts gently projected my awareness into the blueness of the sky and I was up on that fluffy, luminous white cloud, floating along through the sky, feeling free and light, weightless, unrestrained by gravity and physical restrictions.

It was a wonderful feeling to be so free and light. The cloud supported me with a cushiony softness that was unlike anything I've ever experienced. It was as if I was made up of the essence of the cloud itself, yet I knew that my essence—my awareness—was distinctly different.

As the cloud floated along, directed by unseen universal winds, I began to wonder where it was going, but that thought didn't really concern me. I was quite content to just go with the flow, to be completely here now in the present moment, to experience the calm, relaxing feeling of simply floating on the gentle breeze.

Even though the cloud seemed to be drifting in the wind, I knew there was a universal direction it follows, a natural flow of energy, a divine plan, and that this cloud had its own purpose for being, its special mission in life.

I wondered what that purpose might be, so I merged my consciousness with the cloud's consciousness to discover its reason for existence. Inside its misty, ethereal appearance as a wispy white cloud, it had a definite purpose for being. Seemingly floating aimlessly along, it has seen and experienced many wonderful, magical things, and traveled the world in many forms:

Sometimes as the puffy white cloud it is now floating softly on a gentle breeze. Sometimes seeming to disappear and dissipate in the light of the sun, changing its shape and substance, reappearing when it draws moisture from the earth, being nourished from its physical source, and in turn, nurturing the earth with universal energy.

Sometimes it appears as a powerful cloud, rolling and roaring through the sky as it thunders and creates bold streaks of lightning, invigorating and energizing the earth. Sometimes pouring rain, at other times providing a gentle shower of rain, sharing universal nourishment with the earth.

It was always there, in one form or another, fulfilling its divine purpose, just like I'm always here, in one form or another, following my path and fulfilling my divine purpose.

I became aware that even though at times, it seems that my life appears to be like this luminous cloud as it was expressing itself at this particular moment—seemingly drifting aimlessly along, floating through the sky—that there is a unique and very special purpose I have in life, just as every soul has.

Perfectly content to travel softly and easily on this puffy white cloud, I continued to float along, thinking my thoughts and knowing that everything I do and experience is part of a perfect plan I've created for myself, and that all the events in my life have a special purpose, meaning, and reason for existence.

But for now, I only wanted to float through the sky, above the earth, above the physical reality of my existence, being in the blueness, thinking my thoughts and going with the flow, being in the present moment, enjoying the journey of simply being here now, experiencing how wonderful and free this cloud is, and how wonderful and free I am within my thoughts and feelings, and within my spirituality.

I began to think about continuing on my rainbow journey, wondering what experiences awaited me. Suddenly I was standing on the ground again, looking up at the shimmering white clouds in the sky, clearly knowing the mysteries of my mind and the magic of my true spiritual nature, and understanding how infinite and multidimensional my awareness is.

I smiled up at the cloud and to myself, knowing that I've rediscovered some wonderful and magical things. I've rediscovered that my consciousness exists both within and separately from my physical body, and that my thoughts are free to travel on the energy of air inside what appears to be a white, misty cloud of illusion in the sky.

My smile turned into a huge grin of absolute delight that spread joy throughout my entire being. I've learned how to see through my physical reality from a higher, spiritual perspective, I thought to myself. And I've remembered how to fly.

# Chapter Seven

_____ ❧ _____

## *Mystical Music Box*

Continuing to follow my dream on the rainbow path into the color indigo above the sky into the universe, I entered a quiet, warmly-lit room and I sensed—I knew—there was a wonderful treasure here, a special, spiritual gift that drew me into this subdued, sacred place inside my soul.

Looking around, I noticed a small, delicately-decorated music box set with amethyst crystals that radiated the colors of a rainbow. Opening it, I heard a beautiful melody begin to play. The sounds were harmonious and gentle, soft and soothing, inviting me into a peaceful place within myself.

The melody was somehow familiar to me; it resonated with every part of my being. I listened to the peaceful, gentle, soothing melody of harmony that softly flowed into and through my soul.

Delighted, I closed my eyes to more fully experience and appreciate the music as it richly filled every part of the acoustically-perfect room—as it deeply filled all my senses and every part of my awareness with pure enjoyment—as it shimmered softly into and through my body, heart, mind, and soul.

I listened to the music inside myself as it lightly resonated through my body, into my feelings and the thoughts inside my mind, as it played gently through my heart and softly sang into my soul. I completely tuned into the harmony of the tones and sounds of the feelings that the music inspired and brought forth within me.

I somehow knew that the tones and chords I was hearing were the sacred melody of my soul, flowing and resonating deep within me and all around me. The music was filled with the harmony of the vibrations of my soul, bringing me into a beautiful place of inner peace, a place of joy and light. The music was a gentle reminder of my true spiritual essence.

I felt my awareness expanding ever so softly and gently, into the rhythm and tune and melody of my spiritual essence. As my awareness expanded into the music, it became part of me and I became part of the music. I felt as if I was the music, as if I was the melody.

I knew that the music I heard came from a place of memory deep within me, from the knowingness of my soul. The music played the celestial song of the universe—the symphony of my soul. The song sang to me of home, calling to me softly and gently.

This magical, mystical music box played a melody of harmony, peace, joy, and love within me—the natural, spiritual vibration of my soul, inspiring and opening up remembrances inside me. I was in a sacred space of peace and harmony where I was in rhythm and tune with my spiritual essence.

Listening to the melody, I remembered that once upon a time I was a rainbow, then I came back down to earth as a free spirit in physical form and I magically metamorphosed into a butterfly inside my mind; it was a spiritually symbolic way of remembering my true spiritual nature and seeing through physical illusions.

Then I went to the library to read an interesting, informative, and enlightening book about my soul. The book reminded me that I was part of the sunrise and as I began to awaken from a wonderful dream, with traces of this magical melody—this celestial music—playing in my mind, I understood the symphony as it shared the secrets of the universe and the song of my soul.

The music transported me into a shimmering sphere of light inside a magical, mystical dream—a dream within a dream—as I began to enter the color violet at the top of the rainbow. I was in a multidimensional place within my soul, a transparent, luminous space within the universe, within my mind, where every thought, feeling, and experience is real, and they all happen simultaneously in my here and now, in the present moment.

What a concept, I thought to myself. And it all started with a song that shimmered into my awareness, with one verse—the universe.

# Chapter Eight

———————— ⌒ ————————

## *Butterfly Wings*

I found myself in a mystical field of flowers, similar to the meadow beyond the forest, but this meadow vibrated with a special, sacred energy. The meadow was multidimensional, forming and reforming itself in every moment.

It glowed with a shimmering violet light and everything seemed ethereal and transparent, even though it looked solid at the same time. I realized that nothing was really as it appeared to be. Listening to my thoughts, I knew that my true nature was that of a free spirit, dressed in a physical body.

I *knew*—with every part of my knowing—that I am a spiritual being and that I am ever so much more than my physical self, much more than my physical body and my mind.

I *knew* that my soul wasn't limited in any way by physical energies, and that I could expand my awareness and transcend the limits and restrictions of what appeared to be my physical reality.

I *knew* that my soul vibrated to spiritual and universal energies, in tune with nature and the universe, moving in rhythm with knowledge and awareness, in harmony with light. My soul was the universal energy of light, and I knew I could feel and experience my spirit in its pure energy form.

Listening to my thoughts, I compared my soul to a butterfly that's free, moving on shimmering wings of spiritual and universal energies. I knew I could unwrap the physical cocoon of earthly energies and break through the paper-like shell of limited consciousness to fully open up my awareness and set my spirit free.

A movement in a nearby bush caught my attention. I saw a beautiful, rainbow-colored butterfly emerging from its golden chrysalis. Watching its birth, I realized I was seeing something very special and magical.

The butterfly had just emerged into the light and was beginning to open its wings to fly, to explore its new life as a transformed being—as a free spirit. As the butterfly expanded its wings, they shimmered in the sunlight and I realized that, in essence, I am very much like the butterfly.

I felt at one with it and in harmony with the world around me and within me. I began to understand what the butterfly feels like as it frees itself and begins to fly, floating on natural currents of air and energy, enjoying the light of the sunshine all around it, rising and soaring into the sky and through the clouds into the universe.

I felt as if I could rise and soar with the butterfly, in harmony with air and light. I felt as if I could rise and soar into the universe, transcending the illusions of physical boundaries and limits, moving upward through the clouds into the light of my spiritual energies, where my soul is open and free in its true form.

Becoming more in tune with the energies of the butterfly—with the energies of my spiritual nature—I felt as if I was the butterfly and I understood its natural harmony with the universe. Simultaneously I became aware of my natural harmony with the universe; I became aware that I could transcend earthly energies and flow into universal energies of awareness and light.

Bringing this awareness into my mind, I began to feel myself opening up and expanding through the energies of my physical reality, transforming myself into the vibration of my spiritual self.

Blending into my spiritual awareness, I began to feel even more open and expansive and free, much like how I imagine the butterfly felt when it peered through and released itself from its transparent, paper-like cocoon.

As I watched the butterfly fully open up and expand its wings and begin to fly, expressing itself as a free spirit, I began to fully open up and expand my spiritual awareness. Flowing and floating and flying upward into higher vibrations of awareness and light, I became in tune with my spiritual energies and I felt the essence of my soul. As I experienced this, I felt myself—my awareness—blending into the energies of the universe, in harmony with my true spiritual nature.

As the butterfly continued to float and fly, I felt myself floating and flying even higher, emerging and expanding into knowledge and light. The butterfly was free—flying, soaring above the earth—and I was just as free. I was free of the clouds of physical energies, free of the physical illusions I'd enshrouded myself in.

I'd emerged into the energy of my soul. I felt my spirit begin to fly and soar and expand into ever-higher realms and realities of knowledge and awareness and light. Flying and soaring upward, higher and higher, I felt the freedom of knowledge and the light of awareness.

Floating on natural currents of air and energy, I felt my spirit becoming more and more free. As I continued to rise into the true awareness of my spirit, I saw sparkles and shimmers of light—rays of sunshine and the radiance of stars—that illuminated both the sky and the universe. They were vibrating with energy; they felt nourishing and nurturing as they showered me with awareness, as they showered the earth with light.

Absorbing the light and energy, I felt very vibrant and nourished from the universe, very nurtured and energized from within myself, knowing I was really a free spirit and that I was experiencing the energies of the true nature of my soul.

I felt illuminated with the energy of the universe—in tune with my spiritual essence, in tune with the vibrant radiance of the light of the sun—with the energy of my inner truth and knowledge, and the light of my spiritual awareness.

I continued to fly and soar upward, higher and higher, becoming more and more free—transcending the earthly pull of physical energies, expanding into ever-widening horizons of true knowledge and awareness—flying on shimmering wings of illumination and light.

My spirit was free, flying and soaring and expanding into the universe, moving with the motion and rhythm of knowledge and awareness and light.

I was somewhere over the rainbow.

# Chapter Nine

---　∾　---

## *Dancers of the Dawn*

As I began to wake up, I remembered my rainbow dream. Looking through the open window, I noticed it was nearly dawn and wondered what it would be like to be a sunrise. I decided to find out.

I'd read somewhere that sunrises hold a promise of a wonderful discovery—the dawn of a new beginning, the dawn of a new light beginning within you, and that if you could travel into the center of the sun, you'd find a magical treasure inside your soul.

I felt a gentle, warm breeze coming in through the open window and could smell the fresh scent of the morning air and the wonderful aroma of the wet earth recently nourished from the rain.

I went outside to see the sunrise. Looking up at the sky, I saw the rainbow shimmering in the pre-dawn light, offering to be my guide— my way-shower—into the light of my soul.

"Perhaps you're ready to explore and experience the light within yourself as you travel beyond the spectrum of the sunrise," the rainbow said to me. "Perhaps you're ready to completely remember your spiritual knowledge and to rediscover the mystical awareness of your soul."

I wondered if that was the treasure.

Listening to my thoughts and watching their images move in my mind, I remembered when I walked through the forest and reconnected with myself—with my true spiritual nature—and I rediscovered the harmony of the earth with the universe, the harmony between my physical self and my spiritual self.

I remembered the tree that told me the secrets of nature—the secrets of my soul—telling me that the universe was within myself. I remembered the wonderful waterfall that created shimmering rainbows everywhere, and when I looked into the quiet pool beneath, I saw both my physical self and my spiritual self mirrored together in the water. I became aware of how the earth is a mirror of the universe, just as I am a physical mirror of my spiritual self.

I could see a rainbow bridge shimmering in the distance and wondered where that image had come from. I hadn't dreamed about a bridge or walked across a bridge in my dream.

I smiled to myself. Maybe the bridge was in a dream I hadn't dreamed yet, or maybe I had dreamed it a long time ago, as if it had happened somewhere in a dream within a dream.

As I listened to my thoughts, I knew there was a beach nearby because I could hear the sound of the waves gently lapping at the shore. I thought I'd enjoy the sunrise even more if I was there. Arriving at the beach, I found a perfect place to watch the sunrise. Sitting on the sand and looking at the waves as they gently touched the shore, I felt a wonderful sense of peace and harmony within myself and all around me.

I felt as if I was returning to my true spiritual nature. Listening to the rhythmic ebb and flow of the tide, I felt at one with myself and in harmony with the earth and the universe.

Looking across the water and up at the sky, I had a clear view of the horizon as the water seemingly touched the sky. I saw a few misty clouds above the horizon and noticed they were tinged with the early colors of dawn—mauve, then pale orange blending into a beautiful mixture of coral and pink that combined into fuchsia—which colored the bottom of the clouds and splashed across the sky.

The beauty and misty softness of the colors inspired a sense of awe and wonderment inside me as I realized I was seeing more than the colors of dawn, the colors of a new day; I was seeing the colors of a new beginning.

I noticed the sky was getting lighter. As the light from the sun began to shine behind and through the clouds, dissipating the mistiness, I saw the first rays of the sunrise come over the horizon and noticed how the light was mirrored and reflected on the water.

The light of this sunrise was tinged and colored with a wonderful feeling of energy and awareness and clarity. It radiated a vibrant energy as it emanated rays of light in tones and hues of colors and harmony that resonated with the rhythm of my soul. I sensed—I knew, inside my soul—that this sunrise was very special.

I felt the light of the sun softly surrounding me as it gently entered my body, mind, and soul, filling me with universal energy and spiritual awareness. I was vibrating in harmony with the light of the sun, with the radiant energy of the light itself. Feeling and sensing the sunrise with every part of me, I was drawn into the light of the sunrise, knowing that I was ready to remember all my knowledge and fully awaken my spiritual self.

Somewhere within me—within my mind and soul—I realized that I was the colors of dawn, and I began to recognize the light dawning within me. Just as the water had reflected the beginning of the sunrise, I knew that the sunrise in the sky—mirrored within my mind—was a reflection of my spiritual awareness opening up within me, awakening me to the knowledge within myself.

The sunlight sparkled and shimmered on the water, reflecting the light of the universe. Centering my awareness into the light of the sunrise, it became brighter and brighter, illuminating every part of me, filling me with pure enlightenment. I knew that the sunrise was within me and that I was the sunrise.

The sun was above the horizon now and as the sun continued to rise in the sky, I rose with it—higher and higher. The feeling was exhilarating and I felt more alive and awake and aware than I'd ever felt before.

I remembered there was a special place I knew of, a magical place that was beyond the colors of dawn, beyond the center of the sunrise.

Going into and through and beyond the light of the sunrise, I entered that special and most magical place within myself.

It felt as if I was coming home, as if I was returning to myself. I knew I'd been here before in this sacred place inside my soul, where I'd communed with the natural essence of myself, and that I've always known the way to this most special, magical, mystical place.

From within this place, I saw that the sun was beginning to rise in the center of myself, in the center of my awareness, in the center of my soul. As I became more aware of my spiritual essence, a pure white light—a light brighter than the sun—entered into every part of my awareness. I could feel the light vibrating all around me and within me. I could feel this light—this energy of spiritual awareness—vibrating inside my body, my mind, my heart, and my soul.

I experienced indescribable feelings of awe and wonder and total joy as I completely opened myself up and accepted this radiant, vibrant energy of spiritual awareness and enlightenment as it entered inside me, knowing that it had always been part of me.

This pure white light opened my awareness to my spiritual essence and knowledge. As the light became brighter within me, I became more aware of my inner spiritual knowledge—knowledge that is infinite and goes beyond words or thoughts.

I knew this light was the light of my soul—the light of the universe—the light of my spiritual essence vibrating all around me and within me.

This was the light that had shimmered through the mist in the forest and had sparkled with the energy essence of the universe in the rainbow-colored drops of the waterfall. This was the light I saw at the entrance to the library and the light that had shone on the seven steps of the stairway into my soul. This was the light I'd first seen shimmering in the rainbow through the open window in my dream.

I heard my rainbow voice. "Breathe in the light. Become the light and be the light. As you breathe in the pure energy of light, and fully absorb it within yourself, your spiritual enlightenment completely opens up inside you and you become more aware and awake than ever before.

"As you accept the light that is radiating from within the center of the sunrise, from within the center of your being—your soul—you become fully aware of your true spiritual nature and you know that you are the universal essence of light that shines upon the earth.

"The light within you becomes brighter and brighter as the sun continues to rise. Your spiritual knowledge and the awareness of your true nature are interwoven with the rays of sunshine, with the colors of a new day, a new beginning. Your inner awareness becomes clearer and brighter at every moment, as you experience and enjoy the sunrise, as you experience enlightenment within your heart, mind, and soul."

I was in complete harmony with the light of the sun and the light of my soul. The light of the sun and the light of my soul were one and the same. I was the essence of light; my soul was composed of the energies of light.

I had become the sunrise. I was the sunrise. I'd found the treasure; it was the treasure of spiritual knowledge—the gift of my spiritual self awakening within me. Having been given this gift, I wanted to share it.

I saw a golden sun ray that emanated from the sun and shimmered from the sunrise, a golden sun ray that emanated from within me and radiated out from me. I saw how the sun ray originated from the sun and from me, and how it travels from its source to gently touch the earth and to light the way of a beautiful new day.

I noticed that this sun ray sparkled on the water and shone on the beach where I had watched the dawn begin, where I had enjoyed the beginning of the sunrise. I traveled with the golden sun ray onto the beach where I had watched the sunrise—the dawning of the light within myself, within my soul.

I was now sitting on the beach. I saw that the sun was completely above the horizon, above the clouds. The clouds that had reflected the early colors of dawn, and the water that had mirrored the sunrise, now reflected the color of gold—the color of the sun and the color of spiritual knowledge.

The sky was a very bright blue and even as I looked at the clouds that were golden, they changed to a pure white as if they'd absorbed the light of the sunrise.

Looking over the water, I noticed how the sunlight sparkled and shimmered, mirroring and reflecting the light from the sun. I knew that the white light of the universe—the light of my soul—shines and shimmers brightly within me.

I smiled up at the sun, knowing I'd remembered all the wonderful secrets of my soul and discovered the treasure of my spiritual knowledge on the journey I'd just taken beyond the spectrum of the sunrise, on the rainbow path inside my dream.

"Thank you, Rainbow," I whispered, "for showing me and reminding me about the true nature of my soul. Thank you for waking me up to my spiritual self."

# Chapter Ten

—————— ⚭ ——————

## *Awakening*

As I awakened, I looked out the open window and saw that the sun was well above the horizon, shining brightly. I saw the rainbow sparkling and shimmering with light, vibrating rainbow colors all around me. I saw a white mist above the rainbow and heard her whisper to me.

"As you continue to open up and explore your awareness and inner knowledge, and as you more fully remember and awaken your spiritual self every day, it's like the dawn of a new beginning that offers a promise of many new and wonderful adventures and discoveries."

That sunrise was something special, I thought to myself, remembering how the light had shone inside my soul. I felt as if I was still vibrating with light.

"Your remembrance of your inner truth and knowledge, and the awakening of your spiritual self is reflected and mirrored in every experience in your life as you follow this path you're now traveling—a magical, mystical path—a rainbow path."

Maybe my rainbow dream is real, I thought to myself.

"As you continue upon this path, many treasures and rewards open up to you and are offered with every step you take. Spiritual knowledge is the most wonderful treasure of all, because this knowledge leads you to the true awareness of your spirituality and empowers you to express the energy of your soul in all your thoughts, feelings, and experiences."

I wanted to explore more of my spiritual knowledge and wondered what it would be like to travel with my spiritual self. I wondered what my spiritual self could show me.

The rainbow shimmered with light again, showering me with awareness. "Travel lightly on your rainbow path."

I wondered if I was really awake now or if I was still dreaming.

# Part Two

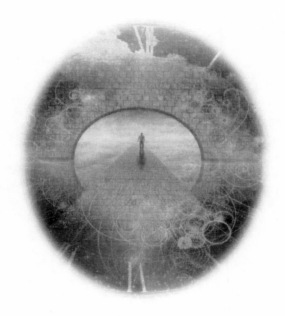

## *Shimmers*

# Chapter Eleven

―――――――――  ᔭᘛ  ―――――――――

## *A Shimmering Rainbow*

The sun was shining brightly as I listened to the rain patter gently on the glass of the open window. As I opened my eyes, I began to recall my dream about following a rainbow path. I looked out the window and saw a double rainbow shimmering in the sunlight. I felt as if I was in a dream within a dream and wondered if I was still dreaming.

I could feel the vibrations of the rainbow sparkling and shimmering all around me, encircling and embracing me. I could feel the energies of the rainbow from within my body—within the center of my being, the very core of my soul—radiating outward from myself. I felt as if I was in a double rainbow—a rainbow of shimmering colors, vibrating in a magical flow and radiance of energy, expanding both inward and outward.

I remembered the white mist I'd seen above the rainbow and wondered what it would be like to travel into the white mist that was shimmering above the rainbow, and then go through the white mist into the universe.

With that thought, I felt my spirit rising through the mist above the rainbow into the white light of the universe. It was like the light of the sunrise, only much brighter. I felt the light vibrating in harmony with my soul, in tune with my spiritual essence.

I felt a love and peace and joy that was completely in harmony with my energies, and I *knew*—with every part of my being—that this is what "home" felt like. I wanted to travel there, to be there.

I heard my rainbow voice speaking clearly in my mind. "You are so much more than a physical being. You are a powerful, radiant, spiritual being of light."

I'm a spiritual sun ray, I thought to myself, remembering when I had traveled into the center of the sunrise.

"There's a bridge of light somewhere over the rainbow, above the mist," Rainbow continued. "Would you like to journey into this multidimensional realm to see what your soul experiences in its pure energy form of light?"

"Yes," I said, wondering where this rainbow path would lead and what I would discover on this journey. I seemed to recall I had seen a bridge somewhere before that was shimmering with light.

Rainbow continued as if she had heard my thought. "A rainbow is the bridge to the universe within you. As you journey into the pure energy of your spirit—as you travel between both worlds to see what your soul sees and to know what your soul knows—you'll discover how to bring your spiritual awareness into every aspect of your life."

It sounded like a dream come true. It was what I'd been searching for—a way to bring my spiritual awareness into my everyday life.

"You'll travel a bridge of light between the earth and the universe, between the physical and the spiritual," Rainbow said, "to journey into your soul and reawaken your spiritual self."

That would be awesome, I thought to myself. I'd never traveled a rainbow bridge before and wondered what a rainbow bridge looked like—if it would look like the bridge I'd seen shimmering in the distance beyond the sunrise in what seemed to be a dream within a dream. I was glad Rainbow was my guide on this journey, my way-shower into and through the light.

# Chapter Twelve

⁓

## *The Rainbow Bridge*

I saw a bridge in the distance shimmering and sparkling with ethereal energy and light, yet the luminous bridge appeared to have physical substance and form. Rainbow had said it bridges both worlds—it spans the earth and the universe, the physical and the spiritual— blending them and bringing them together.

As I walked toward the bridge, I noticed the vibrations of light which formed the bridge were interwoven; the light was in continuous motion. The sparkles and shimmers of light danced together in a synchronous movement—an interplay of motion—with each other, creating a gentle movement, as if a soft summer breeze was flowing through the energy vibrations.

I could feel the energy of light and began to have a sense of anticipation as I wondered what it would be like to walk on this bridge. I saw that the bridge was perfectly formed; it rose up gently in an arch in the center, just as a rainbow arches across the heavens. I saw the handrails on both sides that were formed with tendrils of luminous light.

I couldn't see where the bridge ended; it seemed to stretch into the universe, into infinity, far beyond what my eyes could see. I wondered what I would find on the other side of the bridge and then I knew; it was as if Rainbow was whispering to me—as if I was answering my own thought—that the place my soul called "home" was somewhere on the other side.

I felt Rainbow gently touch my hand, inviting me to continue my journey, to see what was there, what was beyond the physical awareness of my soul.

I began to walk forward, eager to reach the bridge and to travel across it. I had a magical sense of what was awaiting me. I wanted to find my way home. A feeling of wonderful happiness was building inside me with every step I took.

Reaching the bridge. I put my hand on one of the handrails and felt a gentle flow of energy from the bridge in my fingertips. It felt like an effervescent bubbling sensation; it felt pleasant and somehow the feeling was familiar to me, as if I'd experienced this energy before. Then I remembered. I'd felt this same sensation when I'd traveled up the stairs in the library of light.

Stepping onto the rainbow bridge of light between the earth and the universe, I felt the gentle vibration of energy from the bridge begin to radiate upward through me, beginning with my feet. It was the same gentle sensation I had just felt in my fingertips when I touched the handrail.

I knew that this was a magical, mystical bridge and that it could take me above and across the earth into the universe, above and beyond my physical self into my soul. I began to move forward more quickly to explore what was in front of me. The gentle vibration of energy reassured me and invited me to continue to travel across this bridge, this rainbow between the worlds.

I stopped for a moment in the middle of the bridge. I looked back at where I had been. I looked ahead of me and saw a mountain in the distance, rising up majestically into the universe above the horizon into the soft, misty white clouds in the sky. Even though the top of the mountain seemed to be hidden within the clouds, I could see through the soft, white mist into the universe, and knew I could travel up to the top of the mountain.

I looked ahead of me as I walked quickly across the rest of the bridge. There was something about the mountain that my soul wanted to explore. I felt a pull toward the mountain, whether it came from Rainbow or from my soul, I wasn't sure.

I looked at the mountain ahead of me. A beautiful, shimmering rainbow had appeared, encircling the mountain, inviting me forward into the light.

I began to walk toward the mountain, wondering what I'd find, yet knowing at the same time that my journey continued beyond the mountain.

# Chapter Thirteen

## Majestic Mountain

I wondered if I was still on earth or if I was somewhere in the universe, inside a double rainbow. I gazed up at the mountain, at the trees and grassy meadows, the gardens and rivers, and the waterfalls that were touched and highlighted with rainbow colors. I could see a building shimmering with light.

I was standing at the bottom of the mountain in a gently-sloping valley with a softly-winding stream of water in the center. The sun radiated sparkles of light from the water, and everything was lush and green and beautiful. I remembered being here before; I recognized the stream of water that I explored earlier in the magical forest where I'd first seen a glimpse of this mountain.

I wanted to move up the mountain, to explore everything I could discover on this majestic mountain rising up into the universe. I could feel myself—my soul—traveling up the mountain. I began to experience a wonderful feeling of freedom. I felt as if I was standing on the earth and in the sky at the same time.

I saw an opening—an arched doorway—that had been formed between two boulders in the mountainside. It seemed to be lit from within; the glowing light beckoned me inside. I decided to enter, to explore what was in there, and to see where the light originated.

As I entered into the rich deepness of my mind, I saw that the cave was lit with the light of awareness. I remembered the candle meditation on the aura of the flame where I had experienced the energies of my inner self, my higher self, and my soul.

As I became aware of my mind opening up and expanding into the energies of my soul, the light grew brighter and brighter. Sparkles and shimmers of light danced around my awareness. The more I traveled deeper within my mind and my soul, the brighter the light became. It was as if the sun had just come out from behind the clouds.

I could feel the light vibrating inside my mind, inside my soul, filling me with a wonderful feeling of awareness. I felt as if I was beginning to touch my spirituality and wanted to know more about my soul.

As I exited the open doorway, feeling very light and expansive, I felt myself expanding more and more into the sunshine. Breathing in the sunshine, I felt its light moving gently within and through my body, within and through my mind and my soul.

I could feel the bright sunshine all around me. It felt warm on my skin and I allowed the warmth to fill my body, mind, and spirit. Absorbing the sunlight within myself, I felt it permeating every part of me with a very pleasant, gentle warmth and I felt my soul opening up in the light.

Looking up at the sun, I noticed the shafts of light were like a god's eye, filtering through a cloud from the heavens. I felt as if I'd been here before, as if I'd gone on a vision quest to see the light of my soul, yet knew I hadn't traveled that part of my journey yet.

One ray of light was especially bright, and was much larger and wider than the others. It was shining brightly and shimmering with energy. It called to me gently and I decided to see what made it sparkle. As I walked forward into the light, I felt it resonating within me, permeating my soul.

I saw a podium before me, a lectern where perhaps a wise professor or a philosopher would give lectures to students. On the podium, I saw a book of knowledge that was open and waiting for me. I walked over to the book and picked it up, feeling its texture.

I remembered this book from my travels in the light library and yet this book seemed to be growing, expanding, filled with my thoughts and experiences. I opened the book and watched as the words formed images that created the pictures of my experiences.

Cradling my book of knowledge in my arms, close to my heart, knowing that it contained the truth about my soul, I began to travel higher up the mountain into a lush, beautiful green garden, a perfect place of peaceful healing, a spiritual sanctuary of harmony.

Being in the garden and breathing its essence inside me, I felt its vibrations resonating in harmony within and through my body. As I experienced the essence of this beautiful garden vibrating within my mind and my heart, I could feel myself completely opening up my feelings. I felt the garden with my emotions; I felt the garden nourishing my body as well as my mind.

I decided to stay in this garden for a while, to enjoy the peaceful beauty and serenity of nature, to feel the tranquility nurture my soul, and to fully appreciate the flowers that were budding and blooming there. My heart and soul felt complete joy at being in this beautiful healing place of harmony.

As I breathed in the pure, fresh, clean air, and the scent of the greenness and the pleasing fragrance of the flowers all around me, I felt the air and the greenness and the wonderful, fragrant aroma of the flowers in this garden revitalizing and rejuvenating me, filling every part of my body, mind, and spirit with perfect health and harmony.

Feeling completely healthy in body, mind, and spirit, I looked up at the beautiful blue sky above me and saw the expansiveness of the universe. The blue seemed to go on forever. I decided to continue my journey. Traveling higher up the mountain, I felt peaceful and tranquil.

I felt as if my thoughts were words, and my words were images that sprang into action through my feelings. I felt as if I could say and see my thoughts at the same time and knew they were really one and the same, with no difference between the thought and the word. I experienced a wonderful knowing and understanding that the sky and the earth are really one and the same, with no difference between the universe and me.

I felt as if I was completely in tune with the universe, and knew I could communicate with the sky and, in turn, the sky would share its secrets with me. I wanted to listen to what it said to me. I wanted to hear what it could tell me. I wanted to see what it showed me, and I wanted to accept all that it offered me.

I was remembering my soul's wisdom. I could feel my mind opening up even more, expanding into ever-widening horizons that went far beyond what can be physically seen and touched. I experienced an understanding and a knowing that went beyond words and feelings.

I realized I was opening up my mind's awareness, and was experiencing my true spiritual nature. I'd opened the knowing inside my soul, and begun to understand all that was within me. But I knew, at the same time, there was so much more to learn and know. I wondered if perhaps there was a school somewhere in the universe where I could study spirituality.

Thinking this thought, I found myself in a shimmering violet light at the top of this majestic mountain, peering down through the misty clouds at the earth below me, seeing through the illusions that had previously clouded my spiritual vision.

Returning my gaze upward, elevating my awareness and completely opening up my inner knowing and spiritual insight, I saw above the clouds that momentarily seemed to obscure my vision as I simultaneously looked within myself.

As I pierced the veil of awareness that had previously clouded my soul with the illusions of my physical experiences, I completely opened up my mind as my spirit rose into the majesty of my soul above the mountain.

Breathing in this perfect feeling of complete awareness, feeling it permeating every part of me, I felt an awe and reverence within me, deep within my soul. There was a hushed stillness on the top of this majestic mountain that was very calming, very peaceful, very reverent.

I felt as if I was waking up inside my dream.

I wanted to just be here, at the top of this majestic mountain, for a while. I wanted to be completely here in body, mind, and spirit. Breathing in the light of the early-morning rays of sunshine and the pure, clean air, I felt them flowing through me, refreshing me and rejuvenating my spirit. It was like a waterfall of light.

A gentle breeze was blowing; it sounded like wind chimes that made a beautiful sound of music that blended in harmony with my soul. I could feel my whole body resonating with the sound of it.

The music drew me forward. I couldn't quite make out the lyrics but somehow knew that there was a garden inside the music or maybe the music was inside the garden.

I don't know how I knew that; perhaps I simply sensed it in another level of my awareness. I wondered about that. I'd already heard the music of my soul play to me in the mystical music box I'd discovered.

I thought perhaps this dream within a dream was similar, somehow echoing what I'd experienced before as I traveled on my path through the rainbow, yet this dream—this part of my rainbow journey—was very different at the same time, as if I was experiencing more of my spiritual nature in a higher realm of awareness.

The sound of a waterfall drew me forward, deeper into my rainbow dream.

# Chapter Fourteen

⟷ ❧ ⟷

## *Waterfall of Light*

I was in a beautiful, peaceful place in nature that was serene and quiet. I saw a tall oak tree next to a calm, reflecting pond. I remembered this pond where I had seen the essence of my spiritual self shimmering around and through the reflection of my physical self and decided to look further into the calm water.

I saw how the shadows from the leaves of the tree played on the surface of the water and noticed the shadows of the leaves covered only half the pond. The other half shimmered with sunlight that created sparkling patterns on the surface of the pond.

I felt a gentle breeze softly caress me and watched the water as it responded to the breeze by creating gentle ripples on its surface. I knew I was in a magical place, and this pond was very special; it had a spiritual purpose.

Walking closer to the edge of the water, I noticed how the pond reflected the shadows of the leaves, just as it reflected the sparkles of sunlight, and was also reflecting my thoughts and feelings.

I knew the sunlight mirrored all the positive, loving thoughts and feelings I have inside my soul; the shadows reflected all my negative thoughts, feelings, doubts, worries, and fears.

Walking around the pond, I saw there was a place where all the shadows disappeared, where the water was clear and sparkling, pure and clean. I knew, inside me, that viewing the pond from this perspective gave me an entirely new perception of it. I knew the shadows were there only if I saw that they were there.

As I looked at the water in this calm reflecting pond, I knew I could place all my thoughts and feelings there, and they would be reflected back to me in the motion of a soft breeze that created gentle ripples on the surface of the water. The breeze created a soft musical sound in my mind, like harmonious wind chimes. Perhaps this was the music I'd heard before.

I felt drawn to the sparkling, shimmering side of the pond that reflected the light of my soul. And yet I knew there was a positive purpose for the shadows, though I could no longer see them from my current viewpoint.

The water looked inviting, and I knew it was absolutely pure in nature. I dipped my hand into the clear pool of water, wanting a cool, refreshing drink. As I bent down to touch the water, it began to rise up in a magical fountain for me to drink from. I drank deeply from the pure spring of water, knowing I was drinking in its magical qualities, its healing essence, the purity of my soul.

I decided to splash the water on my face, to feel its wonderful coolness and serenity, to feel its magical aura around me. As soon as I had this thought, the water sprinkled me with a gentle spray on my face, returning to the pond in soft shimmers and sparkles of light.

The water that I drank and the gentle spray I felt on my face had a wonderful, rejuvenating effect on me. I felt much happier and lighter than I did before I came to this magical place. A feeling of joy came over me, and I wanted to experience all the magic this wonderful pond had to give; I wanted to experience all the magic my soul has to give me.

I decided to bathe in the water, to bathe in the essence of the light of my soul. At the very moment I had the thought, the water receded from the edge of the pond and rose up in the center, creating a very beautiful waterfall in a rhythm of motion with harmonious, beautiful sounds, radiating and reflecting sparkles and shimmers of light, echoing the light within my soul.

I looked at the waterfall that was shimmering and sparkling with light, knowing it would be as refreshing and magical as the water I drank and the water that sprayed my face. I noticed there was something different about the waterfall that came from the water in the pond.

It shimmered and sparkled in the same manner as the sunlight that was reflected on the surface of the gently rippling water, but the waterfall was not composed of water; it was composed of light—beautiful, warm, inviting sprays and showers of sparkling, shimmering light, reflecting rainbows everywhere.

Somehow, magically, the water had changed into vibrations of light. I wondered if my thoughts and feelings had anything to do with it. Reflecting on my thoughts and feelings, I realized that I was drawn to this side of the pond by the sparkles and shimmers of sunlight that played on the surface, creating a magical melody in my mind that sang to my soul as the soft breeze gently caressed me and created a gentle movement on the water.

I stepped into the waterfall of light, wanting to completely experience it with every part of my being, wanting to be completely in tune with it, wanting to be completely in tune with my soul.

A feeling of total harmony and complete, perfect peace washed over me and bathed me with a waterfall of light, gently permeating every pore of my body, then circulating and flowing through me, filling my entire being with light, completely filling my spirit with that same perfect peace and harmony.

I was completely immersed in this wonderful, beautiful, magical, healing waterfall of light. The light was effervescent and bubbly; it was like bathing in gentle bubbles of energy.

The light gave me a wonderful feeling of being totally alive and completely healthy. The shimmering, sparkling light felt exhilarating, soothing, and peaceful at the same time as it nourished and nurtured me, as it cleansed me in body, mind, and spirit, revitalizing and rejuvenating every part of me.

As I bathed in the healing energies of this wonderful waterfall of light, I felt it healing every part of me as it showered me with health and harmony, peace and joy, as it washed me completely in the pure vibrations of my soul.

I stepped out of the pond, out of the waterfall of my soul's light that was so nourishing and rejuvenating, the light that filled me so completely with harmony and happiness. The waterfall returned to the pond, shimmering with sunlight again.

Stepping back from the pond, I saw the shadows of the leaves again, but this time I understood and knew why they were there. The waterfall of light had gently and completely drawn from me all my cares, worries, problems, ailments, and negative thoughts and feelings, cleansing them and washing them away from me, giving them to the shadows of the leaves, replacing them with beautiful, radiant health inside me.

I saw the pond in a new way, with a clearer vision. Even as I watched the shadows on the pond, the gentle music of the breeze blew all the shadows away, letting the light shine through as it dispersed all the shadows.

The pond was now reflecting my vibrant health, my positive thoughts and feelings, and the essence of my soul. I felt ever so much lighter and happier. I knew the waterfall of light was a reflection of my true spiritual nature.

And I knew I had come to this waterfall of light to bathe myself in the vibrations of my soul's light in order to continue my journey into my spiritual self.

# Chapter Fifteen

҂

## *Multidimensional Meadow*

I was in a field of beautiful, colorful flowers growing wild and free in an open, expansive meadow that was green and lush, filled with life and energy and vibrancy. I remembered the meadow at the edge of the magical forest I had traveled through earlier in what I thought was a dream. I wondered if this was the same meadow and perhaps I was experiencing it in another level of my awareness.

The meadow seemed to vibrate with a special sense of energy that resonated with my soul. The soft, luxuriant green grass felt like velvet beneath my feet. The sun felt warm and pleasant on my face as it touched me with light.

The meadow was filled with thousands, perhaps millions of colorful, vibrant flowers, swaying softly in the gentle breeze. The flowers seemed to go on forever, as far as my eyes could see. Each flower sparkled with light as it shared its wonderful fragrance. I breathed in the scent as it gently wafted to me through the air. I breathed in the peace and harmony of this beautiful, spiritual meadow.

The harmony of the scene beckoned me, calling me to visit and explore further. I felt my soul being drawn into the meadow. I felt a complete peace and harmony within myself, and knew I was perfectly in tune with my soul.

A flower seemed to call to me. I walked over to it and touched it lovingly and gently. I saw that it was a bud just beginning to open up, just as my spiritual awareness was opening up. I watched as the flower continued to open up, petal by petal, as my awareness continued to open up, to bloom and blossom into inner wisdom and knowledge, into the realness of inner knowing and spiritual awareness.

As I smelled the wonderful fragrance of this flower, I felt its vibrant energy and sensed my own spiritual awareness opening up even more inside of me, blooming and blossoming into the vibrations of my soul.

Slowly walking among the flowers, I noticed the sunlight shimmering all around them. The light also seemed to come from within them.

Breathing in their pleasing fragrance as they shared their inner essence with me, I knew they were vibrantly alive, flowing with the natural energy and harmony of life. I felt completely at one with and in tune with nature all around me.

I sat down on the soft green grass in the meadow, wanting to commune with the flowers, with all of nature. As I was sitting amidst the flowers, admiring and appreciating their gentle beauty and quiet serenity, and the vibrations of peace and harmony they were offering and sharing with me, I heard a soft whisper in my mind and realized it was also in the air and all around me.

Listening, I tried to pinpoint the source of the sound, and noticed it was coming from a flower, that the flower was talking to me, and that all the flowers were talking to one another, communicating in their special way.

This seemed a bit surprising to me at first, then it began to feel perfectly natural. I realized I was in a magical meadow where I could hear and communicate with the world of nature, where I could talk to and listen to the flowers, and understand their language.

I remembered that, as a child, I would often talk to the flowers and listen to them as they spoke to me. Looking at the flower that spoke to me now, I saw a little ray of light emanating and radiating and sparkling from the center of it.

At first I thought it was a reflection of sunlight glistening from a small drop of nectar in its center. Looking closely at the flower, I recognized that it looked more like a flower fairy, reminiscent of fairies I'd seen in a garden before.

I smiled to myself, then laughed with pure joy and happiness. The flower fairies I used to believe in when I was a child were **real**. I remembered how I used to play with the fairies who were my friends, how I used to dance and sing and laugh with them.

As I grew into an adult, I placed this wonder-filled time in my memory as a magical game of make-believe, but deep inside me, I knew it was much more than pretend, and I kept this memory in a special place inside my mind.

I wondered why I was experiencing this on my rainbow journey and thought perhaps it was part of reawakening my spiritual nature, then I knew. I wanted to be in that magical world that was vibrantly alive, waiting only for me to fully remember and recognize it—to open up my mind and soul, and become aware of it again.

Rainbow appeared in a ray of shimmering sunlight. "This is more than a special, magical place in your mind—a wonderful memory reopening," Rainbow said. This multidimensional meadow exists in both worlds—the world within of your spiritual knowing and the world around you of your physical, consciousness."

I smiled at Rainbow. I felt as if I was growing my soul into a beautiful garden of awareness and light. I felt as if I was in a garden of harmony, a peaceful garden with lush, green plants and beautiful flowers that vibrated with health and harmony—a garden that created perfect health, balance, and harmony of my body, mind, and spirit, a garden that seemed to be an extension of the meadow I was in.

## Chapter Sixteen

_____ ∾ _____

# *Garden of Harmony*

I was in a very beautiful garden, a garden that seemed to radiate harmony within itself. Looking around, I saw many beautiful flowers and lush, flowering bushes spread among open, spacious, grassy areas. The fragrance of the flowers was lovely and pleasing; the purity of their colors was awe-inspiring.

The bushes and flowers moved gently in the soft, warm breeze, creating balance and beauty within the garden and within my mind. The garden emanated a vibrant feeling of energy, radiant and abundant with life and health.

I felt as if I'd been here before, yet knew at the same time that I was experiencing this garden for the first time. It was similar to the garden I'd enjoyed on the majestic mountain, though this garden seemed to vibrate to a higher level of health and harmony, as if this garden had grown from that garden.

But this garden seemed so familiar, as if I'd been here and had begun to read a book about my soul that was growing by paragraphs and pages with my thoughts.

"Your soul has journeyed through spiritual gardens before," Rainbow said. "That's why it feels familiar yet different at the same time."

I looked at her questioningly. I did seem to recall a garden, but it was more than a garden; there were other gardens connected to it. The memory was vague and misty, as if it had happened in a dream that was interwoven with another dream, or perhaps it was a dream I hadn't dreamed yet.

"There is a garden that every soul travels through on its journey home," Rainbow said.

I wondered if I'd be traveling through another garden on my rainbow journey, then decided to simply be where I was right now. I looked around me, almost expecting to see a book. I wanted to read more of the book.

Everything in this garden vibrated in harmony, in tune with nature. It was very quiet and peaceful here, and the air was clean and pure and refreshing. Breathing in, I sensed the oneness of the garden with nature, and I sensed that same oneness within myself as I began to absorb the harmony and the healing energies of the garden within my body, my mind, and my spirit.

The day was filled with warm, bright sunshine and a brilliant blue sky above me. The light and warmth of the sun on my face and body felt wonderful and relaxing. The grass beneath my bare feet felt soft and luxuriant. The healing colors of the blue sky and the green grass surrounded me, enveloping me with a calm, gentle, soothing, peaceful feeling.

The warmth from the sun's rays began to permeate and radiate through me, filling me with a wonderful feeling of health and harmony. I felt perfectly in tune with nature and with the universal energies of sunlight.

I walked farther within this garden, feeling drawn to a very special place of peace and harmony where I felt most in tune with the healing energies of sunlight and nature all around me. As I entered this special healing place in the garden, I felt completely at peace with myself and totally in harmony with the beauty and serenity all around me.

In this special healing place in this garden of harmony, I could feel the vibrations of energy that were both around me and within me.

As I centered in on the warmth and light from the sun, I could feel the healing energies of sunlight gently vibrating all around me, flowing through me and within me.

I breathed in the sunlight; I breathed in the greenness of the earth and the blueness of the sky. I breathed in the health and harmony of this beautiful garden deeply inside me—into every part of my body, my mind, and my spirit.

I could feel my mind, my thoughts and feelings, and my body vibrating in harmony with the light, totally in tune with both my physical and my spiritual nature, completely in tune with the peaceful, healing energies of the garden.

As I continued to breathe deeply, I brought the peace and harmony I felt within every part of me, and the radiant vibrations of light and health I'd just experienced, into my conscious mind and let them softly flow through my thoughts and feelings, and through my entire body.

I realized this garden of harmony was a special place of healing for me whenever I needed it, much like the waterfall of light was a place of healing. I knew I could return to this garden at any time for healing or if I simply wanted to be in a pleasant place to enjoy serenity and peace of mind.

I felt thankful for the perfect health and harmony I was experiencing in my body, mind, and spirit. I wondered what I would find next on my rainbow journey and looked ahead of me.

I saw that beyond this healing, rejuvenating garden of harmony, there seemed to be a school, a university of some sort. I wondered what a school in the universe would have to offer, then remembered I'd had this thought before when I wanted to open up my spiritual awareness even more.

I heard Rainbow whisper in my mind. "Would you like to attend classes in the universe, where you can remember and rediscover your spiritual knowledge?"

It sounded like the perfect place to study spirituality. I decided to look into it.

# Chapter Seventeen

— ✑ —

## *School of Spirituality*

With that thought, I arrived at a university campus, but it was unlike any school I'd ever experienced on earth. I'd only seen what looked like a university that seemed to be far away from the garden I had been in. How did I get from a garden of healing to a school campus so quickly? I wondered.

"In this dimension, in this realm of awareness, your thoughts transport you the moment you think them," Rainbow replied to my unspoken question.

The school campus was surrounded with a softly-curving arc of light reflecting a majestic sunset of oranges and purples pulsating into the universe. The buildings and trees were bathed in subdued rays of light and hues of color that were vibrating a magical aura of knowledge.

It was a spectacular arrangement of energy. It looked like a replica of an earth university, except it had more ambiance. Vibrations of rainbow-colored energies emanated from within and around the buildings. The school radiated a quiet, peaceful atmosphere, almost sacred. It was a picture-perfect combination of earth elements blended with universal energy.

It looks like a perfect place to study spirituality, I thought, wondering what classes were offered. Not sure where to go next, and feeling a bit out of place, I saw that Rainbow was standing at a podium, giving a lecture.

"Earth is like a school where you learn and are tested through your physical experiences, where you advance and evolve your soul. The universe is also a school where you study spirituality and learn how to express your spiritual nature in all your experiences. There are light teachers here who can help you learn anything you want to know," Rainbow said.

I thought about my spiritual search that had shown me a rainbow path and led me on this journey. I thought about how I'd wanted to find out more about my true spiritual nature; that's why I was traveling this path into spiritual reawakening. I'd often wished that there was a school—a higher place of learning where I could take classes that would help me in my spiritual growth.

"The school of spirituality is a place that exists in the universe, a place where you can remember and rediscover your spiritual knowledge and find answers to all your questions," Rainbow continued. "The curriculum is varied and interesting. There are classes that can expand your soul's awareness. Weekend workshops are offered in any subject you want to know more about."

I wondered what the workshops would be like, and thought a weekend workshop would be perfect for helping me learn more about my true spiritual nature. I wondered what else the school had to offer.

"You can attend special seminars to learn about the spiritual perspectives of living in a physical body. You can take an art appreciation class to see how you *really* create your reality and to learn how to draw more magic into all your experiences on earth. The possibilities are endless," Rainbow said, then looked at me.

"This is a perfect place to learn, to grow my soul," I said.

"Since your soul is grounded in a physical body, you might want to take classes in Time and Space, Reality Awareness, and Energy and Matter to completely comprehend the concepts and to understand the relationship of these subjects on both a physical and a spiritual level, to see how they're intertwined and how the vibrations interact with and influence each other."

I quickly realized that studying spirituality wasn't a crash course or something that could be accomplished over two days in a weekend workshop. It was a life-long journey. I thought about all I could learn here, and I did want to get a higher education that would help me evolve my soul and show me how to pass my earthly and spiritual tests in a better way, with more understanding and insight.

Maybe it was really just a dream or a parallel place in my mind, and I went there every night anyway when I thought I was asleep and dreaming, so it would probably be more fun to become conscious of it. The more I thought about it, the more the idea appealed to me. I was ready to explore this higher realm of learning and awareness, to evolve and advance my soul.

"Let's start with creating your own reality," Rainbow said, leading me into an artist's studio through double doors. "Every soul is an artist who paints all their experiences on the canvas of creation through their thoughts and feelings."

I looked inside the studio. There were tubes and bottles of every color of paint imaginable—some of the colors I'd never seen before. There were thousands of brushes and blank canvasses—tools for me to create all the experiences I wanted to have in my life.

Ideas began to sparkle inside my imagination as I thought about what I wanted to create. I knew this was a special studio and that I could come here whenever I wanted to paint more pictures that would turn into what I experienced on earth when I thought I was awake.

I looked around the studio. It was open and airy and light, illuminated with the universal energy of light. There was a skylight and sliding glass doors around every side that opened into a beautiful garden on one side, a meadow on another side, and a tropical rain forest.

I looked inside my imagination—inside my thoughts and feelings—to see what I wanted to create. Picking up a paintbrush and looking at a blank canvas, I felt magically inspired as I began to paint some of the pictures I wanted to experience in my life. I filled in the details with descriptive images and flashes of insight.

This was fun. I seemed to have a real flair and talent for this. As I allowed the soul artist in me to emerge and come forth, I felt a wonderful power building within me as I realized I could create whatever I wanted, and that I held within my mind all the creative tools I needed to sketch and draw, and shape and sculpt the many images and expressions of my experiences.

Pausing for a moment, I stood back to admire my work. Looking at my partially-completed picture to study what I'd just begun to create and to decide how to enhance the images and what finishing touches and flourishes I'd like to add, I noticed that somehow, magically, the canvas had begun to come to life—to become the experiences I painted.

The images were three-dimensional as they moved and became alive in my experiences. The pictures were living, breathing, being and becoming images and expressions of my thoughts and the feelings that had created them. I saw both the illusionary and the tangible nature of my thoughts, and how they became real first in my mind and then in the physical world.

The pictures—the tones and hues of the colors of the vibrations of my experiences—even as I painted them, were ever-changing in every moment, influenced by my choices, and by every nuance of my thoughts and feelings.

Every action and reaction that I had to the experiences I'd imaged and created caused changes and thereby affected and altered my original ideas, insights, feelings, and experiences, creating new and various expressions to the work of art that is my life in motion.

This is totally awesome, I thought. I'd never realized I had so much power in creating my reality, and how even the merest whisper of a thought became real. I wanted more knowledge. Having that much power was a bit scary and I was glad Rainbow had shown me the school of spirituality where I could learn everything I wanted and needed to know about my soul.

I was feeling a bit overwhelmed with all of this. I put the paintbrush down and looked out the window at a path that led into the tropical rain forest I'd seen through one of the glass doors in my artist's studio.

I could hear the sound of thunder and see flashes of lightning. I've always loved walking through the rain, especially when there was a thunderstorm, so I decided to take a journey through this rain forest where I could search for and find what I was seeking. I wondered if it would be like the magical forest I'd traveled through before.

I wanted to know even more about my spiritual nature. Perhaps a vision quest should be my next step on my journey toward knowledge, toward reawakening my spiritual self.

# Chapter Eighteen

—————————— ✄ ——————————

## *Vision Quest*

I began to follow the path that led me into a tropical rain forest. Beams and shafts of light filtered through the thick canopy of leaves that opened up to the sky in bright blue splashes and glimpses of pure white clouds.

I thought about how I'd begun following a rainbow path when I first began my spiritual search, and now I was looking for even more knowledge. I didn't clearly know what I would find, but knew I'd recognize it when I saw it, then I thought perhaps my vision quest should be open to whatever I experienced on this journey of my soul for knowledge.

I felt totally trusting as I walked forward on my vision quest and knew I would find what I was truly searching for. I continued to go deeper within, deeper within my mind, deeper within my soul. Clouds began to gather. I heard the distant rumble of thunder and saw occasional bright flashes of lightning.

I could smell the scent of rain in the air. It was becoming darker as the rain began to approach, but I felt completely safe because I knew I was guided by my soul. I felt intimately connected with this forest, this place of sacredness I had entered.

I heard a beautiful soft sound, like raindrops. As a gentle rain began to fall softly, I heard the patter of raindrops on the leaves of the trees and the bushes. I saw raindrops dripping from the tips of the leaves and smelled the rich scent of the wet earth as I felt the moisture in the air all around me.

I listened to the gentle patter of the rain on the leaves of the trees, and on the bushes and the flowers. I noticed how the raindrops were clinging to the leaves on the bushes and the petals of the flowers, nourishing and renewing them. I noticed how the rain was gently caressing and cleansing the earth, healing and rejuvenating it.

The rain felt like warm, gentle kisses on my skin. I was completely enjoying this experience of being in this tropical rain forest on a vision quest and walking in this very special healing rain. I felt the rain gently nourishing and healing me as it softly touched my skin. It was like drops of healing rainbow-colored light was inside each raindrop.

The soft, shimmering raindrops seemed to enter inside me—inside my body, circulating through me, cleansing and healing me from the inside out. I felt a wonderful sense of being nourished and renewed by this beautiful rainfall. I closed my eyes for a moment to completely experience and absorb the feel of the rain on my skin and the warm, gentle breeze.

Listening to the sound of the raindrops on the leaves, I became one with the essence of the rain, the scent of the earth, the feel of the air, and with the leaves as they were being touched and nourished by the rain.

Opening my eyes and looking around, I knew I was experiencing the essence of life, the sharing of the earth with the universe, seeing how the universe nourishes the earth, birthing and bringing forth new life, and nurturing the life that is already growing. I became aware of how my soul—my spirit—shares with me and nourishes me.

Even as the rain continued to gently fall, the light from the sun began to emerge, showering the earth with light, and a shimmering rainbow appeared. I felt the awe and wonder and beauty of the rainbow inside my heart and soul.

As suddenly as it began, the rain stopped and the sun burst forth, shimmering and sparkling with light, radiating dazzling rainbows on the water dripping from the leaves. I saw the vibrancy and felt the energy and aura of the forest.

Looking around at the wet, beautiful earth, I noticed all the sparkling rainbows dancing on the leaves of the bushes and the petals of the flowers that were opening up to the light.

Breathing in deeply, I smelled the wonderful scent of the wet earth, freshly nourished and cleansed by this beautiful rainfall of liquid light. Tuning into all these wondrous things around me, I brought them inside me, feeling the joy and harmony of them within my heart.

I realized that the earth and the universe had just blessed me with a beautiful gift—a shower of cleansing, healing rain that washed my heart, refreshed my mind, and bathed my soul.

Continuing on my vision quest, following the path through the rain forest—the path that was leading me within to my soul, to my essence—I came to a tall tree with a door in its trunk, an open door that beckoned me within. I remembered the tree that had spoken to me as if I was an old and dear friend in the magical forest I'd traveled through earlier on my rainbow journey.

Knowing I was completely safe, I entered. Although I expected it to be dark, I saw it was lit with a radiant light from within that was glowing everywhere, illuminating everything it touched with light. It was as if millions of candles were shimmering with light. I felt as if I'd traveled into another dimension of my soul.

There was a special feeling and quality about the light, an ambiance and essence that was both tangible and intangible at the same time; the light opened up feelings within me that were familiar and foreign to me at the same time. Then I began to remember, to know all that is within me, within my soul.

I saw a magical, mystical world opening up and unfolding before me. Gazing joyfully all around me, I knew I'd found what my soul was searching for, and that my vision quest had shown me the way to a special place inside my soul, a sacred space that offered me many treasures and gifts of insight and wisdom, a spiritual place that is my sanctuary, and within this sanctuary I became aware of many things my soul has always known.

Rainbow had been waiting for me. She now came forward to greet me, to walk with me through this wonderful light-filled world of my spirit, and to show and share with me many experiences that my soul was desiring to have in this sacred place within myself, on this vision quest that led me into my soul.

I wanted to continue on my quest for spiritual knowledge; I wanted to reawaken my spiritual self and let the light of my soul shine every day, in and through all my experiences.

I looked at Rainbow, wondering what was next and where my journey would take me. I wanted to explore the light that was shining all around me and within me. I saw a clearing up ahead. I looked up at the sky and saw hundreds of sun rays filtering through the clouds, creating rainbows everywhere.

I wanted to be a sun ray—a spiritual sun ray—and see the light of my soul reflected on the earth, in all my experiences.

# Chapter Nineteen

❧

## *Spiritual Sun Ray*

As I walked into a circular clearing, I knew I was still in the rain forest I'd journeyed through on my vision quest for the light and knowledge of my soul. It was quiet and tranquil here, and I felt very peaceful and spiritual.

I sensed a mystical aura and ambiance in this special, sacred place that brought forth feelings of reverence inside me. I felt as if I was somewhere inside my soul rather than in a rain forest.

A gentle breeze was blowing, caressing me; it seemed to touch me somewhere inside my soul. The trees all around me were softly whispering through the wind to me, as if they had something of great importance to tell me—a spiritual secret.

Listening to the whispers and looking around, I noticed golden beams of sunlight shining through the leaves of the trees.

Standing in the center of the clearing, I looked up to the sky and noticed how the beams of light became brighter, sparkling and shimmering above the tops of the trees as they created intricate and interwoven patterns on the forest floor that were ever-changing in the gentle breeze.

It was as if the gentle touch of the wind and the light from the sun combined their essence to create the mystical ambiance all around me.

I could see and sense that the wind and the light were freer and clearer above the forest. At first I thought it was because there was nothing to block the flow of air or to filter the light, but realized at the same time there was more to it than that.

I recognized the similarity between what the universe was showing me and what I experienced in my life when I went within myself, when I looked within my mind.

I became aware that this was also true of my spiritual awareness, and when I went above the various influences and interferences of my day-to-day activities and the physical energies of my experiences, everything was clearer and brighter, and my awareness was purer, not filtered in any way.

Yet I sensed there was something even more special than this insight that the wind and the light had to share with me now.

The light was warm and welcoming; it beckoned to me and invited me within. As I stepped into a beam of light, it became brighter, and I felt energized and empowered. I had a sense, a knowing within me, that this light was part of me and there is a special quality that I share with the light.

I remembered the beams of light on the majestic mountain that were like a god's eye. And I remembered sitting on a beach somewhere watching the sunrise. I wondered how these were connected, and if it was the same light.

As the wind whispered into my mind and the rays of sunlight energized my spirit, I knew, in a sacred place inside my soul, that I could travel this shimmering sun ray into the center of the sun. I felt as if I had done this before, somewhere in my rainbow dream, yet I knew there was something even more for me to know.

A vague memory began to open up within me that I'd done this before, even before my rainbow dream. As a child, I would often play with the rays of light from the sun and travel the first rays of the sunrise to dance with other spirits of the dawn.

I also remembered that there was a treasure in the center of the sun, beyond the colors of dawn; it was the treasure of spiritual knowledge. Standing in this beam of light, feeling its energy and power, I looked at all the golden sun rays that surrounded me, and the memory began to become clearer in my mind.

I knew the treasure is the light of my soul that opens my spiritual knowledge, and this gift is given to all souls and is meant for sharing. I knew that all I had to do to receive and open this gift was to know it was already mine; it was my spiritual birthright.

Looking upward, I began to travel through the light of the sun ray into the sun, flying and soaring high above the earth into the universe, into the center of the sun. As the spirit of the sun gave me my special gift—the light of my soul, my inner truth, and the complete remembrance of all my spiritual knowledge—the sun told me that the sunrise every morning is a reminder to reawaken my spiritual self and to radiate my light everywhere, every day, in and through all my experiences, to share it with other souls, and with the earth and the universe.

Traveling within the sun ray—within my special essence of light—shining and sharing my light with the world, I noticed that I was now over the clearing in the forest where I began my vision quest—my journey of remembrance and recognition.

Floating down gently through the tops of the trees, I landed softly back on the earth, knowing that the sun—the universal essence of light—was the most special and sacred place I'd ever seen; it was the most wondrous place I'd ever been, and that my soul had just taken a brief journey home to remember and renew its essence.

"As you share your gift of inner light, it will begin to grow brighter and to radiate with its own sacred, unique light to illuminate the world," Rainbow said.

I was a spiritual sun ray, and I recognized the sacred gift I'd received—the treasure I'd always known was within me—is the inner light of my soul, emanating and radiating everywhere, shining brightly. I decided I would let my light shine brightly, every day and in every way.

## Chapter Twenty

ॐ

## *A Dream Within a Dream*

It was morning and I was sitting on a beach watching the sunrise. I felt as if I was waking up from a wonderful dream—a dream within a dream—about traveling a rainbow bridge into the light of the universe where I became the essence of a spiritual sun ray, shining my light upon the earth.

I looked up at the rainbow above me, shimmering through the soft, misty clouds. Reflecting on my rainbow journey, I felt as if I'd discovered a special, magical treasure within myself, a gift from my soul.

I wondered if I was still dreaming. Or if now I was truly awake. I wondered where this dream would take me as I traveled further along the rainbow path I was following.

I wondered if there was something even more for me to discover about my soul, and to completely awaken my spiritual self.

# Part Three

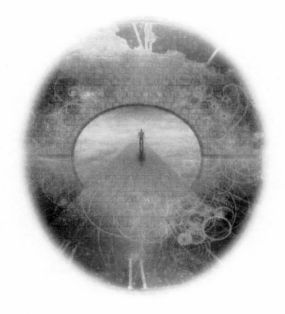

*Soul Gardens*

# Chapter Twenty-One

## *Seven Soul Gardens*

The sun was shining through an open window as a rainbow shimmered all around me. It was morning and I felt as if I was waking up from a dream within a dream about sitting on a beach watching the sunrise and becoming a ray of light when I heard Rainbow whispering to me.

"Would you like to continue your journey on the rainbow path you're traveling to reawaken your spiritual self and find your way home?"

"Yes," I said, knowing that Rainbow knew what was in my mind and what my soul was searching for.

"On the other side of your physical reality, past the bridge of light, in a higher echelon of the universe are seven gardens of your soul," Rainbow said.

I'd heard about the seven soul gardens somewhere in my mind—I thought I'd even caught a glimpse of them before. Then I knew. I'd seen the gardens in the book of knowledge I'd found in the light library—a book that seemed to grow the more I read it.

"Each garden has its own unique vibrations of light and energies; each garden vibrates to a different level of energy and awareness," Rainbow continued. "Each garden offers you the opportunity to explore the multidimensional realities of your soul."

# Chapter Twenty-Two

∾

## *Whispers of Light*

I was standing at the entrance to the most beautiful garden I'd ever seen or been in before. Within the entrance to this garden I could see seven glorious gardens, flowing out and expanding into what seemed like infinity from where I was standing.

I looked into the first garden at the bright, colorful, vibrant flowers swaying softly in the gentle breeze. The colors were magnificent—shimmering and iridescent at the same time. I breathed in the peace and harmony of this beautiful, spiritual place. It was like the garden of harmony I'd recently experienced in what seemed to be a dream within a dream, but this garden appeared to be more than that. The garden beckoned to me, inviting me to visit.

I took a few steps forward, feeling a sense of awe and reverence inside me. The flowers seemed to be whispering to one another as they danced in the gentle breeze that shimmered with light. The whispers seemed to be welcoming me into the garden.

I could smell the wonderful, sweet fragrance of the flowers. I breathed in the beautiful scent. As I smelled the wonderful fragrance of the flowers, it brought forth memories of my soul, stirring deep within me. I could sense the vibrant energy of this garden, and I sensed my own spiritual awareness opening up inside me. I took a deep breath. I was ready to find my way home. I walked into the whispers of light in the first garden. I looked closer at the flowers and saw a sparkle in the center of each one.

I wondered if the flowers here were tended by the flower fairies. I remembered the multidimensional meadow I'd been in earlier and wondered if these flower fairies were the same. I remembered how they whispered to me when I touched the flowers. I looked closer. There was something very different about them.

The flower fairies looked like little angels, with multicolored wings of light. When one landed on a flower, the petals opened up, radiating colors of light all around the flower and the angel who was tending the flower. Or perhaps the angel's wings created the shimmering light, and the flowers responded to the soft whispers of light by opening up to receive the joyful expression of the light. It seemed the light from the angel's wings created the beautiful scent of the flowers.

"The angels here are beings of light and love," Rainbow explained. "They dance among the flowers, spreading happiness and joy. They exist in both the physical and spiritual worlds simultaneously. On earth, their physical counterparts are called flower fairies—nature spirits—who have the ability to change their form."

I remembered the flower fairies I played with as a child, the ones I'd remembered earlier in my dream. It seemed that this was a dream within a dream, within another dream, and the more I dreamed—the more I reawakened to my spiritual self—the more I became aware that there were layers and dimensions of the dream that opened up to me more and more.

I looked around me at all the beautiful flowers. It seemed that joy filled each flower that was dancing in the gentle breeze, radiating vibrations of happiness and laughter as the angel's wings whispered, softly touching each flower, their rainbow auras merging into brilliant, ever-changing colors of light. The angels were also whispering to me, filling me with joy and light as they welcomed me and danced around me. I felt as if I was a flower, filled with light, dancing with the rainbow angels as they shimmered above me.

# Chapter Twenty-Three

---------- ❧ ----------

## *Sacred Song*

I heard a beautiful song in the air all around me as I felt drawn into the second garden. I'd heard parts of this song before when I opened the mystical music box that played a beautiful melody of harmony and home—a symphony of the universe, but the music that now called to me was different somehow—lighter; it sounded like beautiful wind chimes dancing in the breeze.

"Your life is a sacred song; you follow the rhythm of your own soul's music," Rainbow said. "In this garden, you can attune yourself to your own unique soul's melody."

I looked around the garden at the beautiful bushes all around me that were filled with blooms—delicate orchids and multicolored wildflowers, and many kinds of flowers I'd never seen before. Their colors shimmered with a vibrant light and the flowers emanated a wonderful fragrance.

Breathing in, I completely absorbed the colors and fragrances and the energies of the flowers within myself, and—in a way that I somehow completely understood—I became the colors, I became the flowers, I became the fragrance—I became one with their essence.

As I enjoyed their beauty and breathed in their essence, it was as if the flowers were singing to me. I could hear the music inside my mind that resonated perfectly with my soul. I listened to the music of my life, the sacred melody of my soul. As the music flowed through me, I could feel it filling a special place in my soul.

It filled me with harmonious tones of a beautiful melody, softly flowing into, around, and through my soul. The song was caressing and comforting, healing and soothing. The melody of the music brought forth a wonderful feeling of joy inside me. I could feel and hear the rhythm within me that was in harmony with my soul as the melody vibrated through me and within me.

Words were not necessary in the music; I understood the melody perfectly within my soul and knew the pure joy of my soul singing to me in shimmers and waves of light.

I knew the music I heard was the sacred song of my soul, singing to me in harmony. As I recognized the melody, I knew that my sacred song is in every part of me, in every part of my life, and that if I listened, I could hear the harmony of my soul everywhere around me.

I knew that my soul sings to me in the morning, in the colors of a beautiful sunrise of a new day. I could hear it flowing through the leaves of the trees, whispering to me. I could feel the melody in the soft, gentle touch of the wind on my face. I could see the harmony of my sacred song in every beautiful flower as I breathed in its wonderful scent.

The song of my soul caressed and enveloped me every day with its magical melody and sound, touching every part of my life. The soft, gentle, soothing music continued to flow inside my soul. It was the most beautiful sound I'd ever heard.

I listened for a while, then closed my eyes, allowing the music to flow in and through me, filling every part of me with harmony, resonating with every part of my awareness. I felt as if I was one with the music, that the music was me and I was the music.

The music began to softly ebb, lingering like wind-chimes in a gentle breeze, echoing within my soul.

# Chapter Twenty-Four

———————— ❧ ————————

## *Echoes of Light*

When I opened my eyes, still hearing the harmony of the song echoing in my soul, I saw a brilliant light, as if there were millions of candles and echoes of light all around me, and I realized I had somehow entered the third garden.

All the flowers were shimmering in the sunlight, moving gently in the soft, warm breeze. It was as if the flowers were dancing to the melody that softly lingered from the second garden, as if the harmony of the music had overflowed into this garden of light.

The light in this garden was brilliant, warm, and welcoming. The garden was created by light and appeared to be a garden of illumination. The yellow flowers radiated golden rays of wisdom, like rays from the sun, or perhaps they were reflecting the light from the sun.

I felt as if I was part of the light, as if I was the light, and somehow knew I was seeing the light of my soul. The light grew brighter and brighter, expanding and radiating everywhere, emanating rays of light and wisdom.

I remembered feeling as if I was a sun ray, shining my light on the earth and into my experiences and realized I was in a land of light, and this is where the sun's rays originated from. As I was soaking up the rays and warmth and light of the sun, I felt the light and warmth spread throughout my entire body, mind, and spirit, flowing into and through every part of my being.

I looked up above me and saw that the sun was centered in the sky. I could feel the aura and atmosphere of light all around me, and saw how the sun was vibrating with light and love. I felt the radiant light of the sun shining brightly overhead, its rays warming the air, creating its own special ambiance.

I could feel the ambiance all around me—the sun was sharing its radiant light and perfect warmth; the rays of light were warming my body, mind, heart, and soul. I felt my soul opening up to the light— to the light of knowledge. I could feel every thought in my mind opening up and becoming more aware.

I felt completely connected with the light and knowledge of the sun and I knew, somewhere deep within myself, that the source of light from the sun is the same source my soul draws from. I could feel myself becoming the essence of my spirit—radiating and emanating the same golden rays of light that I was receiving and experiencing from the sun.

# Chapter Twenty-Five

♀

## *River of Life*

I saw sparkles and shimmers of light just ahead of me and heard the musical sound of water flowing—perhaps it was a brook or a river—following its course. The sparkles and shimmers of light reflecting off the gently-flowing water drew my attention into the fourth garden.

As I walked into the garden, I could see a clear brook of water flowing through the center. I couldn't see where it began or where it ended, but I had a sense it flowed into a waterfall. The flowing water made a beautiful, rippling sound. The clear, pure sparkling water was filled with lovely, healing, nurturing sounds and I saw rainbows all around me.

I remembered how the sun had sparkled on the gently-flowing stream of water I'd seen on my travels through the magical forest. I wondered if this was the same stream of water I'd also seen at the entrance to the majestic mountain, and if I was now experiencing it again in a higher level of my awareness.

I stood by the water for a few moments to just simply enjoy being in this beautiful, peaceful place. I listened to the gentle, harmonious sounds all around me—to the flow of the water over the pebbles and small ledges in the brook, hearing the song it was singing to me, hearing and feeling the soft sound of the wind as it whispered quietly through the leaves of the trees, creating a blissful, beautiful harmony, as the sounds of this garden spoke softly to my soul.

I felt completely natural and peaceful here in this tranquil garden. The sparkles and shimmers of sunlight on the water seemed to be reflected in my soul.

I decided to walk beside this sparkling brook that made such a gentle, harmonious sound. Somehow, I knew that this gentle stream of water flowed in harmony with my spirit. I listened to the musical sound of the water as it rippled along in the brook, as it rushed and bubbled and splashed along its path, and heard it within my soul.

At times, it was a clear, sparkling stream; at other times, it was a still, quiet pool of water reflecting the sky and the universe, reflecting my thoughts and feelings as I looked into the water.

A gentle breeze, as soft as a whisper of angel's wings, created ripples on the surface of the pond; it seemed to ripple into infinity, into eternity, into the knowledge inside my soul.

# Chapter Twenty-Six

⤫

## *Book of Knowledge*

I wasn't even aware I had entered the fifth garden. I'd simply been following the stream of water—the stream of life—as it journeyed on its way, as I journeyed on my path to spiritual reawakening. I was in a garden filled with shimmering light that spoke to me in whispers of knowledge. It reminded me of being in the light library because I sensed the knowledge within the book I knew must be here, but I was standing in an open garden of light within my soul.

Then I remembered; I'd been here before in this garden, reading a book. I heard a soft, whooshing sound above me and a white gift box tied with a purple ribbon fell from the sky, from the universe, landing softly beside me. I picked it up, thinking it was a gift from the universe and wondering what was inside.

Opening the gift box, I noticed a book inside. I thought it was the book from the light library; it vibrated with the same shimmers of light and I knew it contained wisdom about my soul.

I opened the book, eager to read it, but it appeared to be filled with blank pages. Flipping through the pages, I began to see faint, barely visible images of words. As I read the word-images, they became moving pictures that began to fill in with colors and details; they became more vivid and descriptive the more I placed my attention and awareness on them.

The pictures began to tell me the story of my life, the journey toward my spiritual knowledge, and showed me the many different experiences of my soul as I traveled on my rainbow path through life. I thought about the pictures I'd painted at the school of spirituality and how they'd vibrated and come alive when I put my thoughts and feelings into them.

With every page I turned, the book grew in volume and size as more pages were added, showing me the many facets of my soul. The book described—in vibrant, illuminating images and words—the many avenues and directions my soul has traveled—the paths it has followed and the journeys it has taken. It seemed as if the book was writing itself as I read it, but I also knew I had the power to edit and revise this book, to write and rewrite it any way I chose to.

This book of knowledge showed me many insights into my soul as it offered me the images of journeys I had taken and glimpses of journeys I would travel in the future. It contained images of possibilities and probabilities, and shared with me various imprints of experiences yet to be and offered me choices as to how I'd like to shape and sculpt the future.

The book invited me to listen to my thoughts and feelings, to look within my heart, mind, and soul, into my imagination to write and rewrite the past, present, and future—to change my feelings and experiences with a slight stroke of my thoughts and a soft touch of my emotions.

I hugged the book to my heart. I knew this magical, mystical book was a gift from the universe—a treasure of truth—and that it was given to me to open and read my spiritual knowledge, and to write the story of my soul.

# Chapter Twenty-Seven

❧

## *Wings of Light*

The sunlight shimmered all around me as I entered the sixth garden. My spirit felt free and happy. I felt as if I could fly on wings of light.

I looked around the garden of flowers that was filled with shimmering, iridescent butterflies, floating joyfully on the soft breeze. They reminded me of the angels that had whispered and danced around me in the first garden.

I laughed with pure happiness and delight, loving how free the butterflies were and how joyful they seemed to be playing with the flowers and the breeze.

I felt the soft breeze flowing through the garden as it gently caressed me. I saw an iridescent butterfly perched on one of the flowers. Sunlight shimmered on its wings as the butterfly opened them and began to float on gentle currents of air.

I remembered the birth of a butterfly I'd seen and how it reminded me that I was a free spirit. I remembered how it opened up its shimmering wings and flew into the sunlight, and encouraged me to fly into the light.

I knew that shimmers of my soul were all around me, every day, all the time, and that simply by being open to the awareness and experiences of my soul, I could recognize the light of my soul in even the most ordinary places and mundane moments.

I knew I was very much like the butterfly; that the light of my soul shimmers like iridescent butterfly wings in every moment of my life—in every thought, feeling, and experience I have.

Watching the butterfly floating through the air, I felt as if I was the butterfly, free and natural. I felt the freeness and naturalness of my spirit taking wing and flying through the air, into the azure-blue sky of the universe and the light of the sun.

I traveled on the iridescent, shimmering wings of my spirit to explore the many realms and realities within myself and the multidimensional worlds of the universe around me.

# Chapter Twenty-Eight

_____ ୭ _____

## *Temple of Truth*

As I flew into the universe on wings of light, I landed softly in the seventh garden. I saw violet and purple flowers everywhere. In the center of this garden, I saw a beautiful temple that I knew was the home of my soul.

I entered a violet sphere of light that was gently vibrating and shimmering all around me as I stepped into the place that my soul calls home. Sunlight streamed in through the stained-glass windows, reflecting the multi-colored light of rainbows everywhere.

An energy that could only be called pure, unconditional love surrounded every part of me as it softly flowed through me. I felt loved. I felt an awe and reverence within me, deep within my soul.

There was a hushed stillness within the temple of my soul that was very calming, very peaceful, and I sensed something very ethereal in the violet light that was vibrating and shimmering all around me, as if the light was alive. I was in a still, quiet, peaceful place within myself, within my soul—a special, sacred place filled with light—where I remembered my soul's natural vibration—a vibration of light, love, joy, peace, and harmony.

I felt this vibration completely within and through every part of me. I felt it with every part of my heart, mind, and soul. The feeling was so real and tangible that I could touch it and breathe it inside me.

The feeling was so filled with pure joy that words couldn't adequately describe it, yet I completely felt it and knew it within myself. I was home.

"The vibration of your soul—the light and energy of spiritual knowledge and pure peace has so much joy and wisdom and beauty within it that it naturally desires to express itself," Rainbow said.

I couldn't find the words to speak as I embraced this feeling of wholeness—of love and light within myself.

"In this special, sacred place within you, within the center of your soul, the very core of your being, you have always, in every moment of your life, come from a loving, white light place within your heart, mind, and soul.

"Because you are a spiritual being, born from a divine spark of love, you could not do otherwise, even though at times physical illusions may have prevented your clear seeing of the whole picture and of knowing the reasons for your experiences and actions. Yet your soul was ever-evolving, following its path of inner knowing directed by its inner source to its ultimate destiny—that of love and light."

I was taking it all in, feeling Rainbow's words within my soul.

"Every soul who is now experiencing life on earth is truly a spiritual being of light, just as you are, and their spark of divine love is ever-present, sometimes waiting only for a way-shower—for the light to shine upon them to illuminate the light that is within them."

I knew Rainbow was my way-shower, and that she had showered me with light, and helped me to reawaken my spiritual self. I wanted to let this light within me—the natural vibration of my soul—shine brightly.

I closed my eyes for a moment, to fully absorb the light within myself. I breathed it inside me and felt it permeate and fill every part of me, every part of my heart, mind, and soul.

When I opened my eyes, I saw Rainbow smiling at me. "This is the journey—the rainbow path—that all souls must travel to find the way home."

## Chapter Twenty-Nine

—————— ❧ ——————

# A Rainbow of Light

I heard the rhythmic patter of raindrops softly tapping on my window, gently waking me from sleep. I remembered my rainbow dreams and knew they were much more than a dream. The dreams were real.

I opened my eyes and looked through the window at the sun that was beginning to rise, shimmering its light through a rainbow. It was the dawn of a new day.

I smiled; I knew it was a reminder to let the light of my soul shine. The rainbow light was shimmering all around me and I knew I was truly awake.

"Thank you, Rainbow," I whispered, "for being my way-shower into the light on my journey to reawakening my spiritual self."

# About the Author

Thank you for reading this book. I hope it's been helpful in reminding you of who you truly are… a powerful, spiritual being of light.

Renee Amberson enjoys meditating on the beach at sunrise, walking through the rain looking for rainbows, and being a free spirit. She writes metaphysical books and visionary novels on reincarnation, spirituality, positive mind power, and meditation.

Visit the **Light Library** to browse her books and to look for the light within yourself—https://lightlibrary.blogspot.com.

# Echoes of Mind

———————— ✑ ————————

Box Set ~ *Magical Mind, Magical Life: How to Live a Magical Life, Filled With Happiness and Light* and *Magical Mind Gardens: Grow Your Mind Into a Beautiful Garden of Harmony and Joy*

**Magical Mind, Magical Life** is an adventuresome, interactive guide into opening the magical power inside your mind. It offers you a journey of self-discovery and invites you to open, explore, experience, and understand the natural power of your mind. It's a guide that shows you the way to living a magical life, filled with happiness and light.

**Magical Mind Gardens** encourages you to look within your mind to see the magical power you have to create everything you experience. What you plant and cultivate in your mind grows into what you experience. Filled with 365 magical thoughts, it invites you to grow your mind into a beautiful garden—a place of harmony, joy, happiness, and light—filled with positive thoughts and happy feelings, and watch them grow in your life.

Light Library; ISBN: 978-1-883717-41-4; 294 pages

# Echoes of Time

———————— ∽ ————————

Box Set ~ *Past Life Journeys: Time Tripping Adventures Into Your Soul* and *Past Lives, Future Lives: Mirrors of Time*

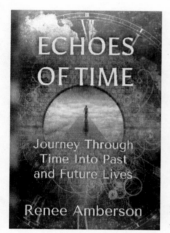

*Past Life Journeys* offers time tripping adventures into your soul. It gives step-by-step directions, interwoven with an in-depth script, for remembering and re-experiencing the events in your past lives, as well as offering sidetracks and side trips—interesting adventures and excursions to explore along the way.

*Past Lives, Future Lives* looks at reincarnation from a simultaneous time-space perspective. It shows how the future interacts with and causes synchronous experiences in the present as it invites you to look through a mirror of time to see an expansive view of the past, the present, and the future—and how these time-spaces affect and alter one another.

Light Library; ISBN: 978-1-883717-19-3; 388 pages

# Echoes of Spirit

∽

Box Set ~ *Somewhere Inside the Rainbow: A Soul's Journey Through the Multidimensional Vibrations of Time and Space* and *Somewhere Over the Rainbow: A Soul's Journey Home*

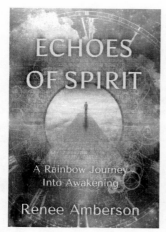

**Somewhere Inside the Rainbow** offers the beginning of a soul's journey through the multidimensional vibrations of time and space. The last thing Amanda ever wanted to do was to experience another lifetime on earth. She can't remember who she is—or even who she was before—and is reluctant to reincarnate. Then she hears a whisper from a rainbow inviting her to follow her dream.

**Somewhere Over the Rainbow** is a visionary novel—part fact, part fiction—about the reality of reincarnation that offers a lighthearted look at the ups and downs of being spiritual in a physical world. Amanda is a free spirit who somehow manages to get herself stuck in the energy vibration of a physical body. Of course, she did it on purpose; nothing happens by accident. She's a little embarrassed to find herself on earth again and wonders how she ended up here when she vowed she'd never reincarnate again.

Light Library; ISBN: 978-1-883717-21-6; 362 pages

Made in United States
North Haven, CT
23 February 2023